Taking Stock

TAKING STOCK

The Calgary Conference on the Canadian Novel

Edited by
Charles R. Steele

Editorial Board

ECW PRESS

This book has been published with the help of a grant from The Canada Council and a grant from the Research Grants Office, University of Calgary.

CANADIAN CATALOGUING IN PUBLICATION DATA

Main entry under title:
Taking stock

Papers presented at a conference held at the University of Calgary, Calgary, Alta., Feb. 1978.
ISBN 0-920802-29-X

1. Canadian fiction — Congresses. I. Steele, Charles Reginald, 1944-

PS8191.N6T33   C813   C82-094208-1
PR9192.2.T33

Cover design by Marie Sherman. Typeset by PhotoComp Services Ltd., Concord; printed by John Deyell.

ECW PRESS
Stong College, York University
Downsview, Ontario M3J 1P3

CONTENTS

Editor's Preface: Charles R. Steele   vii
Introduction: Hallvard Dahlie   1

SESSION ONE: Thursday Morning, February 16, 1978
Robert Kroetsch: Contemporary Standards in the
    Canadian Novel   9
Panel
Barry Cameron   21
W.H. New   34
Warren Tallman   38
Discussion   40

SESSION TWO: Thursday Afternoon, February 16, 1978
Ronald Sutherland: The Two Cultures in the Canadian
    Novel   44
Panel
Naïm Kattan   58
Elspeth Cameron   61
Antoine Sirois   64
Yves Thériault   66
Discussion   67

SESSION THREE: Friday Morning, February 17, 1978
W. J. Keith: The Thematic Approach to Canadian
    Fiction   71
Panel
Henry Kreisel   91
D. G. Jones   93
Laurie Ricou   96
John Moss   99
Discussion   101

SESSION FOUR: Friday Afternoon, February 17, 1978
Eli Mandel: The Regional Novel: Borderline Art 103
Panel
Marian Engel 121
Frank Watt 123
Rudy Wiebe 129
Robert McDougall 131
Discussion 133

SESSION FIVE: Saturday Morning, February 18, 1978
Malcolm Ross: The Ballot 136
Panel
Henry Kreisel 142
Antoine Sirois 144
W. J. Keith 145
Discussion 148

Appendix 150

Editor's Preface

The Calgary Conference on the Canadian Novel, held in 1978, combined formal presentations with informal commentary and discussion. In editing the proceedings of that conference, I have attempted to preserve both formal and informal voices while attempting to extirpate the hesitations, repetitions, and other infelicities of oral delivery, so that I might present a smoothly flowing text. The accounts herein are, therefore, not verbatim. Minor corrections have been made by the authors of the major papers subsequent to their delivery at the conference. The panelists' presentations have been extensively edited by me from conference tapes without, I hope, any serious alteration of meaning and effect. The discussions have obviously been much adumbrated by me, although I have, of course, attempted to report their substance and tenor accurately.

I should like to thank the other members of the editorial board for their support, while exonerating them from any culpability for inaccuracies which may be contained within the following accounts of the conference; the responsibility for any such is wholly and solely my own.

Charles R. Steele

Introduction

HALLVARD DAHLIE

In July of 1955, the first major conference of Canadian writers and critics was held at Queen's University in Kingston. The proceedings of that conference were published under the title of *Writing in Canada* (1956), ably edited by George Whalley, with an introduction by Frank Scott, and this document still stands as a remarkable record of the Canadian literary scene of the mid-1950s. Reading it now, one is struck by the lingering relevance of many of the major issues debated at that conference: the teaching of Canadian literature in our schools and universities, the difficulty of obtaining reliable texts, the absence of a substantial Canadian criticism, the relationship between writers, their publishers, and the public, and so on, but one is at the same time conscious that clear progress has been made on many of these issues in the intervening quarter century. That conference — like most conferences, I suspect — "drew to a close in an atmosphere of befuddled good will," to quote George Whalley, and sounded a concluding prediction that some day "a repeat performance would be offered."

Repeat performances of various sorts and on various scales have indeed been held, most notably at U.B.C. in 1956, at Fredericton in 1970, at Calgary in 1973 and 1978, at Banff in 1978, and at Regina in 1979, but of these only the Banff conference has to date had its proceedings published.[1] It is easy to see in retrospect that, though these conferences all had a life of their own, and bestowed much immediate pleasure and instruction upon their participants, there is nevertheless no doubt about the overriding importance of getting the proceedings into print as quickly as possible, so that a cumulative and permanent record can be built up of the development of literature and criticism in this country. Thus, even though a fair amount of time has now elapsed since The Calgary Conference on the Canadian Novel took place, all its organizers are indeed pleased to see their efforts assume a tangible, permanent form and, like George Whalley, hope that our document will well serve future generations of students and critics of our literature. My careful re-reading at this stage of the papers, discussions, and responses so competently assembled and edited by my colleague Charles Steele thoroughly reinforces the opinion frequently expressed by many participants at that time: that the ideas generated by the conference were too important to be allowed to fade into post-conference nostalgia and distortion.

It is true, of course, that not all aspects of the conference received a unanimously positive tribute at the time, and the risk still remains that the Calgary conference will forever be known as the one that produced the controversial list of a hundred novels. In retrospect, one might wish that the list had been debated as "the hundred most frequently taught novels," rather than "the hundred best" — though that might have incurred the risk of its receiving no attention at all. It is instructive, however, to look again at Malcolm Ross's circular of November, 1977, which accompanied the official ballot, and to recognize the utter rationality of his requests: first, that we help select a list of a hundred novels which "can be recommended as central to any study of Canadian literature"; second, that we list our own choices "for the *ten* best Canadian novels yet written"; and third that we list "ten Canadian works of literature *of any genre* (including literary criticism) which [we] consider most indispensable to the study and appreciation of our national literary heritage." Only academics, I am sure, could make a controversy out of such non-controversial requests, but make it they did, and in the process somehow transformed a useful working list into a prescriptive canon. This aspect of the conference earned flashy and ephemeral headlines, it is true, but it is also true that requests for the list kept coming in from all across Canada and from overseas long after the immediate furor of the occasion had died

2

down. This fact, I believe, reflects an underlying feeling sensed by organizer and participant alike: that it was necessary to articulate and celebrate the stature that the Canadian novel had by virtue of its own intrinsic qualities already achieved, but which, for various reasons, had not been sufficiently recognized and proclaimed.

This conviction was expressed by Bill Keith in his paper, "A Thematic Approach to Canadian Fiction," one of the five keynote addresses to the conference: "Canadian literature has now attained a sufficient solidity and stature that we can invoke high standards without any fear that the subject might succumb to the process." Sceptics might argue that the very fact that such a statement had to be articulated is proof that Canadian literature has not attained this state of development, and in this sense they might share to some extent Bob Kroetsch's frustrations at being unable to be as confident about his assertions as Leavis was about his. The problem, however, does not necessarily lie in the substance of Canadian literature, but both in the conditioning processes we all have been subject to in our perception of that literature, and in the sceptical nature of our times, as it were: as Kroetsch implied, and as Barry Cameron explicitly pointed out, Leavis was able to make his dogmatic pronouncements at a time when it was still respectable and acceptable to do so, when assumptions about writers (and not only dead ones) could in large part be prescriptively handed down to the reading public. In the case of Canadian fiction, on the other hand, both the situation and the problems are of a different order, as Kroetsch cautioned us: ". . . we are engaged in a kind of pantheon-making among the living. We occupy the most treacherous ground." It is a tribute to the participants involved in our conference that neither writers nor critics avoided this treacherous ground, and throughout the five sessions "the conflicts of perfervid devotion and chilly good sense,"[2] to borrow George Whalley's recollection from the Queen's conference, raged vigorously, if not always conclusively.

What the conference articulated above all was the maturity and richness of Canadian fiction, and even if it did not begin to achieve the ambitious fourfold objectives set out by its organizers, it did provide a national forum for the discussion of these objectives. In poorer times fictionally, a consensus might well have been reached simply in self-defence, but there was a comfortable feeling here that at last no apologies and no explanations had to be offered. Opinions clashed, to be sure, but they didn't cancel each other out; participants complained about the list of novels, but as often as not to decry the absence of this or that novel, rather than to wish the list undone; and the ghost of Leavis kept reminding the participants that while it would be nice if we could say conclusively "the great Canadian novelists are . . . ," we can at least state with conviction at this point that there are a number of significant Canadian novels that *are* central to the study of our literary heritage, and that is a respectable achievement indeed.

The general reader and literary scholar alike should be both encouraged and enriched, not only by the keynote papers themselves, but by the conflicting opinions which these papers generated. They should find that their own puzzlements will at the very least share a respectable company, and may even to some extent have been resolved. Following Eli Mandel's paper on regionalism, for example, Rudy Wiebe argued convincingly against the very notion of regionalism in literature, which won me over until I reread Frank Watt's statement that the Canadian novel is "going deeper and deeper into more varied, more particularized explorations of meaning in vital, regional settings" — a prognosis which is supported by such novels as Ethel Wilson's *Swamp Angel* and Jack Hodgins' *The Invention of the World* (both singled out by Keith in his paper), and by at least three of Wiebe's own novels. Similarly, both Doug Jones and John Moss take Bill Keith quite properly to task for his misconceptions about thematic criticism, though their rebuttals do not disprove Keith's major argument. Complementary opinions, too, like Warren Tallman's delightful anecdotal gloss on Kroetsch's paper, or Elspeth Cameron's sensitive extension of Ronald Sutherland's thesis, help us achieve new perspectives on a particular book or on a general trend in our fiction. My point of course is that both our fictional scene and our attendant critical scene are now so confidently established as part of our cultural fabric that we do not have to worry either about our inability to hear a Leavis in our midst, or about any need to subscribe to pronouncements about the fiction of other countries. The novels which ultimately emerged on the select list of the "top ten" did not of course enjoy the unanimous support of all those who participated in the conference, but no one would dispute the fact that they reflect an artistry and a substance that characterize a mature and confident fiction.

[1] Richard Harrison, ed., *Crossing Frontiers* (Edmonton: Univ. of Alberta Press, 1979). A summary of the 1956 U.B.C. conference was included in *Writing in Canada*.

[2] George Whalley, ed., *Writing in Canada* (Toronto: Macmillan, 1956), p. x.

SESSION ONE: Thursday Morning, February 16, 1978

Robert Kroetsch: Contemporary Standards in the Canadian
   Novel
Panel
Barry Cameron
W. II. New
Warren Tallman
Discussion

Contemporary Standards in the Canadian Novel

ROBERT KROETSCH

F. R. Leavis, in *The Great Tradition*, proposed to do for the English novel what we propose, here, to do for Canadian fiction. He would establish the canon. With an enviable confidence he began his book, "The great English novelists are Jane Austen, George Eliot, Henry James and Joseph Conrad . . . ."[1]

Literature and literary values have undergone enormous changes in the twenty-five years since Leavis collected his controversial essays. The very idea of "canon" has come into question. What a novel is, is open to debate. The idea of evaluating at all is dismissed by some distinguished critics. There are even those who ask what an author is or what he does. And yet, over the past few weeks, I've found myself going back to Leavis' book — if only to see how he could be so confident.

This paper is a record of my reluctance — and of my need — to locate/discriminate the canon of Canadian fiction. I can only trust that my fumbling will point towards the success of others.

Leavis states his criteria on the second page of his book. He will start "by distinguishing the few really great — the major novelists who count in the same way as the major poets, in the sense that they not only change the possibilities of art for practitioners and readers, but that they are significant in terms of the human awareness they promote; awareness of the possibilities of life" (p. 2).

Art and life coming together in the novel. It sounded easy. Even as I read I began to frame a sentence in my mind — "The great Canadian novelists are F. P. Grove and Malcolm Lowry . . ." — I hesitated, realizing I had chosen two writers who were not native-born, one who might not be Canadian at all. But again — Leavis listed two English novelists who weren't English-born. I tried to fill out my sentence. Margaret Laurence, surely, gives us an awareness of the possibilities of life. But how does one evaluate her sense of form? Marie-Claire Blais, on the other hand, manages to experiment with form, but does she not explore the *limits* of the possibilities of life?

I went back to Leavis. His concern with art became an uneasiness with either experiment in form or undue stress on style — became something of a dismissal. His concern with "the possibilities of life" turned into the phrases, "moral preoccupation," "moral intensity," "moral earnestness."

At that point, Morley Callaghan began to climb my list. Callaghan, it struck me, is a religious moralist, while MacLennan is a secular moralist. But what is best about both those writers is their transcendence of their own moral postures, their ventures into the realms of energy, myth, origin, contradiction.

I ended up suspecting — feeling — that "moral intensity" is not a criterion by which to judge Canadian fiction. Canada is a moralistic place; any people as compulsively interested in drinking, screwing, and making money — and I applaud all three, though not necessarily in that order — as are Canadians, are sure to be moralistic. But moral? As the little boy said when his mother told him there are people starving in China — "Name one."

The most genuinely moral novel in Canadian literature is Malcolm Lowry's *Under the Volcano*. Written about a drunk, and by a drunk, it asks only the unanswerable questions. Those are moral questions as opposed to moralistic questions. The minute you ask answerable questions, you're beat as a novelist. What's the point? people like to ask. The minute there's a point, you've lost the art. Art may well be instructive as well as entertaining. But the instruction is not prescriptive. It is perceptual. And that takes us into the dread realms of language and imagination, or the possibilities of art.

But first a little more on moral intensity.

F. P. Grove is a writer of great moral intensity because he is himself a sham, a liar, a criminal, a fraud. Out of the terrible pressures within himself, he creates moral predicaments and explores in violent and new ways the connections between autobiography and the novel, between fiction and reality.

Rudy Wiebe, much influenced by Grove, flirts with the moralistic. He is saved from the cloying stink of piety by his own huge energy, by the temptation of violence, and by his erotic relationship both to language and to the process of writing. Ernest Buckler — an immensely private and troubled man, when he is not being sentimental (and that too may finally be part of his vision) — makes of the flirtation with morality a huge novel: *The Mountain and the Valley*. But I am not persuaded that either of these splendid talents is powered by a moral preoccupation. Wiebe works out of a radical perception of history, especially in *The Temptations of Big Bear*. Buckler works out of a radical perception of the self as both self-creating and self-destroyed.

Leavis, in *The Great Tradition*, sets up what a Structuralist would call a binary pattern. Life versus art, if you will, yes; a distinction that neither Lowry nor Grove would tolerate. He sees the binary opposition as resolving itself into a moral stance on the part of the author. The secularization of this idea, in post-Leavis criticism, led to the concept of "sincerity." "Care" in the novel is what matters. Instead of conscious art we have conscience art.

I suspect that the moral criterion appears long after something else. Moral criticism takes its doctrine from outside the literature. But what is the non-moral and integral source; how name it? For the moment, at least, I'll settle for what the Plains Indians (and Sheila Watson) called it: Coyote.

But I still haven't grasped why we make room on the crowded shelf of fiction for one book, and not for another. How and why do we insert a particular text into the row of existing texts, or into what some might call the supertext?

I turned from Leavis to a work by D. H. Lawrence. His small book, *Studies in Classic American Literature*, when it appeared in 1923, gave a validity not just to a book or an author but to a whole new body of writing. Though an English novelist himself, his "evaluation" inserted American literature onto the shelf of world literature. In the introductory and generalizing chapter of his book, which is called "The Spirit of Place," Lawrence says: "It is hard to hear a new voice, as hard as it is to listen to an unknown language. We just don't listen."[2]

What applied then to American literature applies now to Canadian fiction. It is hard to hear a new voice, as hard as it is to listen to an unknown language. Where does the voice come from? What is it trying to tell us? Why do we resist hearing?

Lawrence attempts an answer. "Out of fear," he says. "The world fears a new experience more than it fears anything. Because a new experience displaces so many old experiences. . . . The world doesn't fear a new idea. It can pigeon-hole any idea. But it can't pigeon-hole a real new experience. It can only dodge" (p. 2).

Canadian readers have certainly been committed dodgers. One can hardly blame them, watching the many critics and professors and publishers who lead the retreat. Malcolm Ross has been one of the rare few who would listen to the new voice, the unknown language.

For a while I was tempted to argue that the only way we can avoid dodging, at this point in time, is by accepting everything. After the vacuum, the plenum. Take the "Official Ballot for the Selection of Canadian Novels" (and how Canadian that is: please, no blood, no loud noises, no pissing in each other's boots), add the glaring omissions, and let every reader exist in an existential situation. Let each reader read everything and decide — if he or she believes in that kind of decision. Or better still, don't decide at all: embrace a Heideggerian "letting be" against the "will to power." At a time in our history when we have a neurotic distrust of centralized power of any sort, it might be better to let the individual read without direction — supported, of course, by The Canada Council.

But the other side of me — and the tension between idiosyncrasy and the communal good, between individual pleasure and communal concern, is always there — the other side of me insists that, essentially, one of the ways in which we build a culture is by selecting and elaborating a few texts.

The Christian and Jewish worlds are built pretty much on the elaboration of a single text. High English culture of the nineteenth century, it might be argued, was built on the elaboration of a few classical texts. A handful of authors from the nineteenth century are basic to the elaboration (and the strength, the direction) of American literature — which takes me back to Lawrence and his recognition of the American pantheon.

The catch is that Lawrence, for all his talk of the new, was dealing with texts that were at least sixty years old. Critics, sixty years from now — when the oil has been pumped from beneath Alberta, and Calgary is a wonderfully quaint and decadent city — critics will no doubt smile condescendingly at our judgements. For we are engaged in a kind of pantheon-making among the living. We occupy the most treacherous ground. It is well, in this predicament, to look to Lawrence's principal criterion. He says,

> Art-speech is the only truth. An artist is usually a damned liar, but his art, if it be art, will tell you the truth of his day. And that is all that matters. Away with eternal truth. Truth lives from day to day, and the marvellous Plato of yesterday is chiefly bosh to-day. (p. 2)

I find myself agreeing, often, with Lawrence. I am willing to let the new experience displace many old experiences. I am willing that truth live from day to day as must the rest of us.

The novel, by this view, is a kind of weather report. The weather is not a moral issue (except, on occasion, in Alberta). The weather is a matter of skin and crops and what to wear today and should we go out to the lake or should we start the swathing or should we cover the tomatoes. The novel as weather report is a matter of here and now, of time and place. It demands of us an exact measuring and an exact response. We must, each morning, free ourselves from sleep and into perception. The act of perceiving what is actually there is possibly the most difficult act of all — because we come to it with memories, with expectations.

The paradigms established by other literatures are immensely satisfying to many of our readers, to tenured professors, and to book reviewers who wish to write a review without reading the book. To a handful of serious critics and writers — and to a growing audience — the paradigms of other literatures patently and blatantly don't enable us to respond to our weather.

The accommodation, the breaking of forms and the creation of new, the recognition of new language and new content, took place in American literature in the nineteenth century. One hundred years later we are having a parallel experience in Canada. Now we can look back to Thoreau and Hawthorne and Melville and ask: What is the characteristic shape or concern of an American book? The answers are coherent to us — the ideas of Eden found and destroyed, the testing of extremes in language, the blending of Romance and Realism, whatever.

But now we ask: What is characteristic of a Canadian book? How do you know, when you read a new book, that it could only have been written in a particular country — that it is the art-speech of a particular *place* called Canada?

So far we have answered chiefly in terms of content or theme. This seems to be typical of a new literature, be it Nigerian or Australian (think of Patrick White) or Canadian. We face the problem of asserting a *significance* in a culture that is profoundly uneasy about self-consciousness and about its image in the eyes of others. Canada is for the moment — or recently has been — a country in which literature is expected to be conservative. The audience wants old-fashioned characters in old-fashioned stories — an audience for which good language means no expressions like shit or cock. This makes for a literature written by writers who on one hand long for approval; they grope for the great tit of security. On the other hand, they long to be artists; they long to discover the integrity of their own language and their own forms.

In the course of the writers' own hesitation, the act of criticism is made to assume huge and noble proportions. This is true in cultures that are in certain ways at an opposite extreme from our own (France and America come to mind; but in those countries the resultant criticism is highly theoretical, not thematic and moral). The writer is seen as a passive force. He is merely the agent of his culture and of his language. He does not speak; he is spoken through. He is the mouthpiece, the amanuensis. He surrenders or loses his authority. This figure is not to be confused with the writer of old who asked the Muse to inspire him. This new and hesitating writer is without authority. The writing, as we say, writes him.

In this situation the creative book — the novel or the poem — is merely the speech act of the society. A book must be interpreted, written *about* rather than written — or, again — decoded.

We live in a time of significant and lively critical activity in Canada — and please understand that I take the critical act to be a serious and essential act. I take the critics I'm going to name to be serious and significant critics.

Warren Tallman, with his essay, "Wolf in the Snow: Modern Canadian Fiction," sets a standard of critical writing that, by its very effectiveness, began to define a canon. His expression, "uncreated childhood,"[3] offers a terrifying and exact insight that must inspire more recent writers on our culture like Dick Harrison and Laurie Ricou. Doug Jones and William New and Ronald Sutherland and John Moss have published a veritable pod of books whose substance is *substance* — and in the process may already have defined a canon: W. O. Mitchell, Margaret Laurence, Robertson Davies, Margaret Atwood, Mordecai Richler. . . .

But a critic of the critics — someone like Barry Cameron (and, especially in Toronto: Ann Mandel, Rosemary Sullivan, Barbara Godard) — might insist that the criticism more clearly honour the text. They would or will be joined in their protest by the writers who see the writer not as agent, but as something almost the opposite — the inventor of the world.

Edward Said, in his critical study, *Beginnings*, speaks of the European novel and "the desire to create an alternative world, to modify or augment the real world through the act of writing. . . ."[4]

I suspect that the Canadian novel subscribes to the same ambitions — for all the talk about the documentary in Canadian writing. And I suspect that those novels that survive the supreme critical test — that of time passing — first of all create and modify and augment.

Jack Hodgins has recently published a fine novel that is called simply, *The Invention of the World*. Robert Harlow's *Scann* (along with its protagonist) has the same ambition. Rudy Wiebe has a comparable aim in *Big Bear*, for all the attention to history. By this criterion, *Under the Volcano* is a supreme novel, demanding as it does our submission to the book's landscape and characters and length and language.

Some authors invent the world through a series of books: as in the work of Margaret Laurence, Robertson Davies, or Mordecai Richler — novelists who, book by book, would seem agents of the world, not its creators.

As I entertain the notion of the novelist as inventor, I find myself returning to the idea of plenum. All possibilities begin to exist. Our novelists are many; they invent many worlds. I come back to a modified version of that original "letting be."

The fiction shelf is crowded with existing books. The writing of a novel itself becomes a critical as well as a creative act. A new novel criticizes existing novels, is criticized by them. One must ask then: What Canadian novels can one *not* avoid in the writing — or the reading — of a Canadian novel?

I recognize that I run perilously close, here, upon the rocks of mere autobiography. But I do insist that in a very real sense we make books out of books. The paradox and the terror is always that: the need to invent out of the already invented. Get too close to the already invented and you are mere imitation (and often a best-seller). Get too far from the already invented and you have fallen from your precarious perch on the Tower of Babel.

I say Canadian novels, recognizing all the while that I have a life-long debt to and possibly war with Joseph Conrad, that I reluctantly and hopelessly admire *The Great Gatsby*, that I would like to have been Thomas Hardy but can't resist the comic vision. And further, I recognize that there are important novels that I haven't yet read — such as *A Strange Manuscript Found in a Copper Cylinder*.

Those novels that I/we shouldn't/can't avoid:

1. The novels of historical value. Richardson's *Wacousta* is such a book. It acts out — forecasts — Frye's bush-garden premise. It confronts the suppressed sexuality that is so much a part of Canadian fiction — and, I am told, of Canadian life. It relates that suppression to the Gothic. And the impulse towards the re-telling of stories — the very notion of literature as a re-telling — is there. And even the failure of the language is instructive — the problem of the new voice, not only trying to make itself heard, but trying to hear itself.

2. Then there are the sub-literary texts. The Canadian writer as explorer or traveller. The stranger, the alien, the outsider — seeing a new world with old eyes. Seeing and failing to see. Alexander Mackenzie, for instance, gives us a version of maleness that chills the blood. We learn from his writing versions of space, of geography, of character, of absence. The self that is us and yet no longer us. The awe-full not-seeing of the European which finds expression in a novel as recent as Brian Moore's *The Luck of Ginger Coffey*. The first immigrant stories, now to be rivalled by the novels of back-migration, *The Manticore* showing the way.

Second, there is the Canadian writer not as British traveller but as English lady. Please: no sex. Thank you, Queen Victoria. And all her proliferating descendants. A vast national crossing of the legs. Put your prick away and get the crop in: o paradox, o paradox. The

16

homesteader's wife as go-getter. Let's *civilize* this *place*. The male as that special kind of ineffectual comedian: Haliburton, Leacock. The men out in the barn, in the beer parlor, in the bush, on the boats — pretending they haven't been whipped. And the questions, always: What is a novel? What is a fiction? And the ladies' recurring question: Why, in all this civilization that I've created, do I want to be eaten by a bear?

3. The region as novelist. Sinclair Ross, Buckler, Grove: in the sense that they are written by place, by weather. The novelist as weather report. And we wait to read their lives almost as much as to read their novels. Grove, especially and centrally, becomes a fiction. Stegner, in *Wolf Willow*, that central book, recognized the connection between self and fiction in regional writing. We ask now if Ostenso really wrote *Wild Geese*; the novelist becomes a part of the fiction. Gabrielle Roy, in *Street of Riches*, begins her fiction with the novel disclaimer: "Certain events in this narrative took place in real life. . . ."[5] But I leave it to Eli Mandel, himself one of the fictions of this region, to draw the map of this weather.

4. Dear Novelist: Please make us feel at home. The naming. The domesticating. Margaret Laurence. Robertson Davies. Mordecai Richler. The Prairie dweller. The Ontario WASP. The urban ethnic. Each in his own nagging way names us into safety, into at-homeness. Versions of Genesis. A victory of humanism — when some of us are sceptical about the humanistic tradition. But home is always a place of quarrelling — and a place of departures and returns.

5. Dear Novelist: Please give us the courage to be afraid. Wiebe: the fear of fiction. Ondaatje: the fear of fact. In both, necessarily, a subsumed eroticism. In each: the courage to say that the name doesn't stick. The courage to say we are not at-home. Both furiously engaged with the language that at once announces and subdues their fear. Both, curiously, tempted by the myth of reality as it adheres in story.

6. Writing as the *subject* of writing, not just a means. It may be that, sixty years from now, the discoveries will be made in this category. For the moment, there is so much half-assed prose in Cana-

dian writing, so much surrender to subject matter. There are writers for whom it would be an embarrassment, even a disgrace, to write an interesting sentence. There is something in our literature that is a linguistic equivalent to the national crossing of the legs.

Against this humdrummery we have a few writers who are somehow totally aware of what language is. In Montreal, we have Clark Blaise (*A North American Education*) and Ray Smith (*Lord Nelson Tavern*) — possibly out of their experience as a language minority — writing with an exact awareness, though in totally different ways, of how a language is its own subject. The short story form gives us also the best work of two other language-aware writers: Matt Cohen in *Columbus and the Fat Lady*, Dave Godfrey in *Death Goes Better with Coca-Cola*. The experimental novel has an uneasy success in Graeme Gibson's *Five Legs*, a marvellous success in Audrey Thomas' *Blown Figures*. But I'd like to push the notion of language experiment further. Roy Kiyooka's *transcanada letters* may be a novel. Grove's *Over Prairie Trails* may be a novel. Rudy Wiebe's *Big Bear* may be a novel. George Bowering himself may be a novel.

But the two obvious masters in the writing about art — taking seriously (and metaphorically) the creative act — are Ross and Lowry.

Sinclair Ross confronts for every Canadian — not just every Canadian writer — the temptation of silence. That is, the temptation to abandon language in its most demanding implications. Warren Tallman writes of *As for Me and My House*: "Philip's need to escape from the isolation drives him to art. But just as he can find no terms under which he may act as a self so he can find no terms under which he may act as an artist. . . . The novel is a study of a frustrated artist — actually, a non-artist — one unable to discover a subject which will release him from his oppressive incapacity to create."[6] The curious Canadian temptation to paint (draw) rather than to speak.

Against that temptation of silence, we can read Lowry's temptation to write the final book. The book that will contain everything. Malcolm Lowry's dream of *The Voyage That Never Ends*: his dream of a final book that would free us not from but into writing. The unfinished book that we are always reading and never finishing: because every story needs a story to explain, to tell, how come the story was told. The endless beginning.

7. Out of that dialectic — out of the works of Ross and Lowry — we come to the artist as shaman. The artist, possibly sick himself, who becomes healer of himself and of others. The sick healer. The lying truth-teller. The loony wiseman. The wide-awake dreamer or the dream-life of himself, of others, even of his society. Sheila Watson, in *The Double Hook*, murdering one by one the daughters of Victoria. Mother, who is my mother? And A. M. Klein on the other side of the continent — risking his own madness in the shaman-ride — asking: Daddy, who is my daddy? Back migration again. The nightmare of the past as dream, the dream as nightmare. Both writers breaking form, breaking into form. Joined by Howard O'Hagan in *Tay John*, who visits other ancestors. Joined by Roch Carrier in *La Guerre, Yes Sir!*, making comic war against war. All of them, like Marie-Claire Blais, turning the mad shadows into story.

And that is the novelist's predicament, summed up ideally in the predicament of Scheherezade, in the *Arabian Nights*.

Scheherezade must go on telling stories — stories that compel the listener — or that same mad and sane listener, that king, her husband, will put her to death. She must invent life, literally, by telling stories.

I suspect that the serious novel, the "good" novelist, is always in that predicament — and we make classics of the stories that have that sense of being compelled — nothing less. We might ask: How does she shape a story? What are her themes? By what critical standards does the king judge?

Whatever the answers, we know that she is the artist. She is invented by the world and she is inventing the world. Each night she is both virgin and experienced lover. She loves language just slightly more than she does truth, or morality, or even the king's cock. She lives between nightmare and dream, in a world that we name the world.

And she, the teller, as the telling goes on, becomes the tale. . . . As we too . . . . As we too . . . .

[1] F. R. Leavis, *The Great Tradition* (New York: New York Univ. Press, 1963), p. 1. All further references to this work appear in the text.

[2] D. H. Lawrence, *Studies in Classic American Literature* (New York: Seltzer, 1923), p. 1. All further references to this work appear in the text.

[3] Warren Tallman. "Wolf in the Snow: Modern Canadian Fiction," in *Godawful Streets of Man: Essays by Warren Tallman, Open Letter*, 3rd. ser., No. 6 (Winter 1976-77), 131.

[4] Edward W. Said, *Beginnings: Intention and Method* (New York: Basic, 1975), p. 81.

[5] Gabrielle Roy, *Street of Riches*, trans. Harry Lorin Binsse, New Canadian Library, No. 56 (Toronto: McClelland and Stewart, 1957).

[6] Tallman, p. 137.

Response

BARRY CAMERON

I really have no quarrel with anything Robert Kroetsch has said, but I would like to approach the issue of contemporary standards in the Canadian novel from a different angle, picking up a few of his points later and developing them in a different context. Perhaps I should state clearly at the outset the premises on which the following remarks are grounded. The problems of critical methodology and evaluation with which we seem to be increasingly preoccupying ourselves in the study of Canadian literature have nothing to do with the nature or quality of the literature itself. Because of the literary explosiveness of the past decade and a half, we have suddenly found ourselves face to face with a recognizable and relatively large body of literature with which we are forced to come to terms. It is obvious to even the least perceptive among us that Canadian literature is "no longer," as Northrop Frye has said in the most recent edition of the *Literary History of Canada*, "a gleam in a paternal critic's eye."[1] In fact, were it not for the literary activity of the past decade and a half, I doubt whether we'd all be here today. Rather, the problems lie squarely in the area of critical theory, for we indeed lack, as Malcolm Ross has said, "a meta-criticism," or "*ground*," which is a "precondition of an authentic practical criticism."[2] Despite my awareness of the risks involved, I am going to try to rise or descend — depending on one's point of view — toward that ground. The nature of a conference with such blatant evaluative aims demands such an attempt, I think, and I see no effective way of speaking about standards in the Canadian novel without recourse to a discussion of critical theory. My approach will necessarily involve speaking somewhat abstractly, but, towards the end of my remarks, I hope to offer some concrete directives for applying the theory I shall propose.[3]

Consider, first of all, the excruciating difficulty, if not madness, of what we have agreed to do here in Calgary during the next three days. I quote from the Conference programme:

> The Conference on the Canadian Novel will provide a forum for discussions which have four main objectives: to provide a norm which can serve as a curriculum reference for teachers of Canadian literature at all levels; to suggest to publishers selection criteria and titles for future Canadian fiction series; to establish standards for future scholarly editions of Canadian novels; and to provide a guide for Canadians who are interested in the masterworks of their national literature. The final result will be the identification of those novels which have established themselves as Canadian classics.

To provide a norm, to suggest selection criteria, to establish standards, to provide a guide, to identify classics — boys oh boys, as we say in New Brunswick, what bold faith the organizers of the Conference have in us and in the presumed validating powers of what they would seem to hope will be an institutionalized verdict! It would be easy, tempting, of course, to dismiss such ambitious aims, as I'm sure some already have, on the ground of the subjective relativism of all value judgements, a stance with which Robert Kroetsch tells us he has flirted: since there is no such thing as an objective or absolute value judgement, "let each reader read everything and decide" for himself, "or better still, don't decide at all." It may be in fact that such large evaluative aims will ultimately have to be qualified in terms of subjective relativism, but there are other, more compelling reasons for questioning the possibility of fulfilling these aims meaningfully.

As E. D. Hirsch points out, when David Hume in his 1757 essay, "Of the Standard of Taste," argued that no specific criteria of literary judgement could be "fixed by reasonings a priori," he was nevertheless "able to recommend" instead institutional criteria "founded upon experience: a literary work should be deemed excellent which mankind has long judged to be so, or which the intellectual aristocracy of the present day judges to be so. Hume placed his confidence in the uniformity of human nature and the observable consensus among well-educated men," "the majority rule of the best judges." Hume's pragmatic principle for determining standards may be called "institutional" "because, like all institutions, its authority rests upon social agreement. . . . In Hume's day the best judges could be recognized and accepted; implicitly they could be institutionalized on the analogy of the Supreme Court, the French Academy, or the Pope."[4] Unfortunately, Hume's position on standards simply does not fit either the sociological or historical situation in which the study of Canadian literature finds itself in the late '70s. It does not answer the Arnoldian question of what is or should be the function of criticism at the present time; and, like Arnold and others, I believe that criticism should — and does — shift its function from age to age, generation to generation, a point to which I shall return later.

Take, for instance, Hume's first criterion, what at one point in the essay he succinctly calls "durable admiration." Hume in 1757 could comfortably assert that "The same Homer, who pleased at Athens and Rome two thousand years ago, is still admired at Paris and at London,"[5] even as F. R. Leavis in 1948 could — in the phrase of Robert Kroetsch — "with an enviable confidence" proceed to establish the great tradition of English novelists. Both Hume and Leavis could do so because, despite other criteria, they at least had temporal distance from the objects of their evaluation, which had been sifted and weighed on the scales of time.[6] Because ours is a young, emergent literature in Canada, because many of the novelists we might wish to evaluate are alive and well and some of whom if not living then visiting in Calgary today, such distance and the psychological objectivity attendant upon it are just not possible. We are, as George Woodcock has so precisely put it, living "*beside* the archetypes of our own tradition" (emphasis added).[7] For better or worse, moreover, we are everywhere as critics and teachers confronted with the personalities, the persons, of our writers. (Take a good look around; maybe you're sitting beside an archetype.) Ya want a novelist or poet to read to your class? Sure, all ya gotta do is pick up the phone — dial-a-writer sponsored by

The Canada Council. No matter what his criteria of evaluation —
aesthetic, say, or cultural-nationalist — such a situation hardly allows the critic much objectivity. Frye has said recently that "It may
be the end of the century before any real coherence will emerge
from our cultural pattern: so far we are confined to what Eliot
would call hints followed by guesses."[8] That may very well be so,
especially with respect to Canadian literature as a whole, but there
are nevertheless, I shall suggest, some quiet critical activities that
we can perform in the meantime.

We don't fare any better with Hume's second criterion for
determining standards either: the institutionalized joint-verdict
among well-educated individuals of the present day, which may
sound like a simple process but is far from it. In order to qualify for
a seat on Hume's intellectual bench, a critic must exhibit "A perfect
serenity of mind, a recollection of thought, a due attention to the
object" of evaluation, a "delicacy of imagination," a lack of
prejudice, and freedom from "the continual revolutions of man-
ners and customs" (pp. 316, 317, 321). To exercise judgement in
this state of mind, moreover, Hume says, requires practice. One-
time or hasty judgements made in December when an envelope ar-
rives from a tabulation centre in Toronto are likely to be wrong or
superficial.[9] It is not, then, merely a matter of calling for a majority
vote. Do we have in abundance, are we unequivocally, critics with a
"strong sense, united to delicate sentiment, improved by practice,
perfected by comparison, and cleared of all prejudice . . ." (Hume,
p. 320)? If anyone out there thinks he or she fully qualifies, would
you please stand up and identify yourself; we need you up here on
the dais.

Despite the illusion of the hierarchial institutionalized nature
of this conference, moreover — complete with a hit-parade chart
and a disk jockey who's going to announce the top ten for us on
Saturday morning or, to mix metaphors, with a converse Catholic
Index and Pope — we have really been "For some centuries now,"
as Hirsch points out, "literary protestants without Pope or priest-
hood," though some, both inside and outside Canada, have tried
hard to establish the Frygeans as a reputable order of priests.
"Prophets and sects we continue to have, like the other Protestants, but nothing resembling" a Papacy (p. 111). We have neither
recognized nor recognizable, neither accepted nor acceptable,
judges. In fact, such institutionalized hierarchical evaluation is not
possible for any literature in the '70s; it is even less possible for

Canadian literature given the circumstances I described a moment ago: ". . . in the modern world no single hierarchy of values is privileged. We lack the institutionalized authority or the genuinely widespread cultural consensus which could sponsor truly preferential criteria in literary criticism. Absolute evaluation requires an absolute; it requires a universal church. But the actual world of literary evaluation has been for some time now a protestant world where preferential criteria are in fact only the preferences of a sect" (Hirsch, p. 122).

What I have argued so far might be called a sociological-historical explanation for why institutionalized privileged criteria of evaluation are not possible at the present time. I also want to offer some philosophical or logical reasons for rejecting the idea of absolute privileged criteria since my own position on the evaluation of Canadian literature evolves from these reasons — since, paradoxically, I am in fact going to advocate a set of privileged criteria for Canadian criticism at the present time but not necessarily for eternity — and, once again, I draw on the thinking of Hirsch.

Hirsch makes an extremely useful distinction between the "meaning" and the "significance" of a verbal text and between the "interpretation" and "criticism" of a text. He writes, ". . . the term 'meaning' refers to the whole verbal meaning of a text, and 'significance' to textual meaning in relation to a larger context, i.e., another mind, another era, a wider subject matter, an alien system of values, and so on. In other words, 'significance' is textual meaning as related to some context, indeed any context, beyond itself" (pp. 2-3). "Meaning," however, "is not restricted to conceptual meaning. It is not even restricted to mental 'content,' since . . . it embraces not only any content of mind represented by written speech but also the affects and values that are necessarily correlative to such a content" (p. 8).[10] Meaning is "meaning-for-an-interpreter"; significance is "meaning-as-related-to-something-else." "Meaning-for-an-interpreter can stay the same although the meaningfulness (significance) of that meaning can change with the changing contexts in which that meaning is applied" (p. 80).[11] Verbal meaning is the exclusive object of interpretation, and significance is the proper object of criticism. Now, what I want to suggest in a moment, in terms of these distinctions, is that as commentators on Canadian literature we have not been paying enough attention to interpreting texts as such and that we have been paying almost exclusive attention to only one context or kind of significance, which some see as privileged — namely, Canadian consciousness or identity.

Value judgements or value preferences, as distinct from the values that are necessarily correlative to the very act of cognition involved in interpreting any verbal text, are, Hirsch says, matters of significance, for "significance names the relationships of textual meaning, and value is a relationship, not a substance. Value is value-for-people" (p. 146). There are four sets of evaluative criteria that have evolved in the study of literature over the years, one set clearly extrinsic to literature and three that appear at first glance to be intrinsic but only one of which is absolutely intrinsic. The first, extrinsic value criteria, judges a work as good or bad "on the grounds of its external relationships" (p. 114). Plato's instrumentalist view of literature, for example, invokes such extrinsic criteria: "A work of literature shall be judged good if and only if it is good for the state. What is good for the state is to be defined thus and thus, and what is bad thus and thus" (Hirsch, p. 115). The second, evaluation-through-genre (Aristotelian, Chicago critics), judges a work "good to the extent that it fulfills the intrinsic imperatives of the kind to which it belongs . . . and bad to the extent that it fails to fulfill those generic imperatives" (p. 115). The third, *sui generis* criteria restricted to the individual work (Crocean critics), judges a work good or bad in terms of "the particular goals of the work itself" or in terms of adequacy: "how fully does the work accomplish what it is trying to do; how expressive is it of its own intent?" (pp. 115-16). The fourth, "broadly generic criteria, restricted to a large genus that includes many different species of works, but excludes some species" (p. 164) — Brooks and Warren, the Yale critics — posits a species such as literature, poetry, or art; defines "the proper excellence of that species in a generally applicable way"; and then evaluates "individual works according to the degree they fulfill that proper excellence" (p. 116).[12]

Hirsch demonstrates convincingly that none of these sets of evaluative criteria is inherently or logically privileged, even the *sui generis* criteria, which are the only truly intrinsic set ("What difference does it make how well an aim is achieved if it is not a valuable aim?" [Hirsch, p. 118]). Take, for example, the fourth set, the broad genre theory of literature so prominently and persuasively advocated over the last forty years by such critics as Cleanth Brooks: ". . . criteria like complexity, maturity, richness, compression, tension, and so forth, are (except when they happen to coincide precisely with the author's intention) extrinsic criteria. Their sanction comes entirely from the religious, moral, and aesthetic standpoint which sponsors such criteria as estimable values. They are not sanctioned by anything intrinsic to the nature of literature" (Hirsch, p. 121). Even genuine aesthetic categories of evaluation are intrinsic only to aesthetic enquiries, not to the nature of literary works, for not all literary works have an aesthetic interpretive meaning. One can study novels as "literature," as "art," but to do so is not logically a privileged or intrinsic critical-evaluative approach to novels — though it may be valid — for novels are verbal texts whose genus (all other verbal texts) and species (other novels, which is not really a genuine Aristotelian species) include works that do not have an aesthetic interpretive meaning.[13] "The only activity attendant upon criticism that has a privileged character is the construction of meaning, which is no necessary part of criticism. One must, of course, understand a linguistic work in some degree before discussing it, but one's understanding need not be the main subject of one's criticism. And even understanding (i.e. the construction of original [or authorial] meaning) as contrasted with misunderstanding has only an ethical and not an ontological claim to privilege" (p. 135).[14]

If there are, then, no inherently or logically privileged criteria in literary evaluation, there nevertheless can be objectivity and accuracy. Depending on his purposes, a critic may make an ethical choice to establish, say, "national consciousness" or "national identity" as his criterion of evaluation. If he makes clear what that criterion means — and that's the rub — then his judgement of a novel in those terms can be just as valid and absolute as a judgement drawn on the basis of some other criterion. Now, I might be disinterestedly willing to accept such a criterion as privileged provided that the critic could convince me that his criticism takes into account a cognizance of the interpretive meaning of the text and that there was some observable consensus about the definition and significance of his criterion. In other words, because the choice of criterion is an ethical, not a logical, one, the critic's case rests upon his rhetorical powers of persuasion about the value of his approach. As I have implied in these remarks, and stated polemically elsewhere,[15] I have not found myself convinced by criticism of Canadian literature that posits either national consciousness or cultural patterns as criteria of evaluation. For reasons I have already presented, consensus on what our national consciousness might be and an objective perspective on the shape of our cultural patterns do not seem possible. More often than not, too, whether it concerns itself with theme or image or both, such criticism tries to present an overview by dealing with a variety of texts, but because of this conglomerate quality, the interpretive meaning of individual texts is frequently ignored or misunderstood. Such criticism does not, in my view, fulfill the function of criticism at the present time: I don't think we are really ready for an overview on the basis of any criterion; we are clearly at the stage of hints followed by guesses, which can, let me stress, nevertheless be an exciting place to be.

This brings me to my own ethical choice of criteria, the critical tasks on which I think we should be concentrating at the present moment. Let me state my position baldly: we should be concerned first with accurately interpreting individual texts — with illuminating, because it now seems so necessary, original or authorial meaning — and second with critically applying our understanding of such meaning to our writers' use of verbal forms and language. For it seems to me, and to many others, that that is what our writers themselves are consciously concerned with — form and language. As Eli Mandel has said — and may say again tomorrow — the writer's task at the present time in Canada has become "an increasingly sensitive articulation of his literary tradition — not to write up the experience of the country but to articulate the forms of its fiction."[16] Robert Kroetsch is right to view me as a critic who does not see the writer as a passive force, as merely "an agent," but rather as an active "inventor of the world," of culture and of language.[17] The sort of thematic criticism currently being practised in Canada, however, does assume that the writer is implicitly a spokesman or agent of a society and that literature's main function is to present visions of society, and such criticism looks at language not for itself, but primarily as a referential or representational tool that points to something beyond or outside language. But verbal stances or attitudes or visions in novels can only exist in verbal structures; they do not derive from the physical, geographical, or social environment in which the writer lives, but from the particular verbal forms and conventions, the language, that a particular society employs to speak of its physical, socio-political, psychic, and spiritual life in that place. Somewhat like Frye, I suppose, I believe that the narrative structures or informing myths of literature are not merely recurring structures of poetry, drama, and novels, but also constructs of the human imagination and memory, thus constitutive not only of literature, but of society and the human mind as well. We imagine everything and everyone; we remember everything and everyone; we invent everything and everyone — including ourselves: insofar as experience is available for comment, insofar as it has meaning, insofar as it is present to us — immediately in front of us now — it is available only as fiction (*fingere*: to shape or to make); and identity, the definition of ourselves and of our relationship to things outside ourselves, is the supreme fiction.

Individual novels intensify, elevate, draw attention to, our fictionalizing habits of forever arranging and rearranging our experiences and others' into narratives, and they invite us to focus on the structures of narrative, the fictionalizing process itself. External reality — the world — cannot really be mimetically recorded, cannot be known without displacement, because it is in constant flux, and so reality, the world, must be invented (*invenire*: to discover, to devise, to acquire). We can know reality — and therefore ourselves — only through language; we invent our world and ourselves through language, through novels. The critic's function, then, is not to bridge art and "life," but to analyze the components of invented worlds and their relationship — thus to create new worlds. As Richard Poirier in *The Performing Self* says, although "all expressed forms of life, reality, and history have a status different from fiction as it exists in novels, poems, or plays, they are all fictions nonetheless . . . . To talk or to write is to fictionalize. More than that, to talk or to write about novels or poems or plays is only to re-fictionalize them. [Kroetsch's view of criticism as an "elaboration" of the text; Mandel's view of criticism as a ghost "story"] . . . Insofar as they are available for discussion, life, reality, and history exist only as discourse, and no form of discourse, as Santayana insisted, can *be* what it expresses; no form of discourse can *be* life, reality, or history."[18] Literature, then, is, as Robert Kroetsch has said, an unnaming, a demythologizing, a retelling, a reinventing — destroying, reshaping, the old story to tell the new one — and even as we invent the writer, the writer invents us, the reader.[19]

What all this means is that I find those fictions most exciting that are concerned with "the possibilities of art," that dislocate and reinvent the conventions of the novel and conventions of language, and we are fortunate in Canada to have several novelists who face this challenge in important ways. The most interesting of these, in my view, are Wiebe, Hood, and Kroetsch. There are, of

29

course, enormous differences among these three writers — if there weren't, I doubt whether I'd be interested in them as an ordinary reader — but all three ask, demand, that their readers unlearn the established conventions of modern fiction: beginnings, endings, point of view, character, and plot. All three dislocate narrative conventions by intermingling narrative voices, levels of fiction, points of view, narrative modes and forms, styles, sentence syntaxes, places, and times in order to dislocate, to reinvent, our perspective on experience and fiction. All three have reinvented the function of the novel — redefined it in more capacious, elastic formal terms grounded in an awareness of man's fundamental and habitual psychological activity of fictionalizing and, in so doing, have reinvented Canadian experience and the Canadian past. All three see the novel less as artifact than as an "enabling act," for both the writer and the reader, that acts out "the play of possible meanings."[20] For Wiebe, Hood, and Kroetsch, novels are not artifacts concealing or revealing ideas but "fictional histories" in a Dantean sense signifying ideas, values, and figural relationships; and, like Dante, all three are concerned with a comprehensive "telling" of the sacredness and the profanity of human existence and, through that telling, attempting to reconcile the two.

I have drawn attention to these three writers in particular because their canons are relatively large and because they deserve the epithet "major" when one speaks of Canadian novelists in general. But there are other Canadian writers who warrant our esteem for some of the same reasons — I think immediately of Jack Hodgins and Michael Ondaatje. One can find all sorts of other motives for reading and studying the work of these and other Canadian novelists, but I suggest that, at the present time, it is by concentrating on the forms and on the language of their fiction that we might "invent" who we really are.

NOTES

[1] "Conclusion," in *Literary History of Canada: Canadian Literature in English*, ed. Carl F. Klinck et al., 2nd ed. (Toronto: Univ. of Toronto Press, 1976), III, 319.
[2] "Critical Theory: Some Trends" in *Literary History of Canada: Canadian Literature in English*, III, 161.

[3] Much of what I shall say here is informed by the views of E. D. Hirsch, Jr., in his two important books on hermeneutics, *Validity in Interpretation* (New Haven: Yale Univ. Press, 1967) and *The Aims of Interpretation* (Chicago: Univ. of Chicago Press, 1976).

[4] E. D. Hirsch, "Privileged Criteria of Evaluation," in *The Aims of Interpretation*, p. 110. All further references to this work appear in the text.

[5] "Of the Standard of Taste," in *Critical Theory Since Plato*, ed. Hazard Adams (New York: Harcourt Brace Jovanovich, 1971), p. 316. All further references to this work appear in the text.

[6] I am reminded of a remark of T. S. Eliot's in his essay "What Is a Classic?": ". . . it is only by hindsight, and in historical perspective, that a classic can be known as such" (*On Poetry and Poets* [London: Faber and Faber, 1957], p. 54).

[7] "Introduction," in *Poets and Critics: Essays from* Canadian Literature *1966-1974* (Toronto: Oxford Univ. Press, 1974), p. ix.

[8] "Conclusion," in *Literary History of Canada*, III, 329-30.

[9] In late November 1977, Malcolm Ross, on behalf of the organizers of the Conference, sent a three-part ballot to "all those who are being invited to attend the Conference," asking the recipients to choose the hundred most significant Canadian novels (ranking each "Major," "Significant," or "Of Secondary Importance"), the ten best novels, and the ten works of any genre considered "indispensable to the study and appreciation of our national literary heritage." Subsequently — before, during, and after the Conference — many people — writers and critics, participants or otherwise — if they did not object to the very idea of such a tabulation, then they objected to the failure to allow the recipient to indicate his criteria of selection. On what grounds did Margaret Laurence's *The Stone Angel* top both the hundred most significant and ten best lists?

[10] Meaning is an affair of consciousness — either the readers', in which meaning is variable, or the author's, in which meaning is determinant: ". . . the nature of a text is to have no meaning except that which an interpreter wills into existence. We, not our texts, are the makers of the meanings we understand, a text being only an occasion for meaning, in itself an ambiguous form devoid of the consciousness where meaning abides" (Hirsch, pp. 75-76). Meaning, however, is not merely "a paraphrasable or translatable 'message,' but embraces every aspect of representation, including the typographical and phonemic, which an interpreter construes" (Hirsch, p. 79); and because ". . . an intentional object cannot be dissevered from a species of intentional act . . . subjective feeling, tone, mood, and value, are constitutive of meaning in its fullest sense. One cannot *have* a meaning without having its necessarily correlative affect or value" (Hirsch, p. 8).

11 "An interpreter could, for instance, find the following to be variously meaningful: 'The cat is on the mat,' depending on whether the cat has left the mat, on whether he likes cats, and so on. The point is not that an interpreter must apply meaning to changing contexts, but that he could do so and still be able in every case to construe his text as representing an identical meaning" (Hirsch, p. 80).

12 Thus an inclusive set of interpretive and critical questions which one could ask of a particular text — and which I have suggested as a guide to reviewing in an editorial in *The Fiddlehead* ("Running Risks: The Art of Reviewing," No. 112 [Winter 1977], pp. 3-5) — might be as follows: 1) What is the writer's rhetorical purpose as manifested in the text? To answer this question is to interpret, to determine, meaning, presupposing that meaning can reside only in consciousness. 2) Has the writer fulfilled that intention? 3) If so, how has he fulfilled it? To answer these questions is to invoke *sui generis* criteria of evaluation. 4) Has he done so well? To answer this question is to consider the work in terms of sub-generic and broad generic criteria. 5) Was it a worthwhile intention? To answer this question is to move into clearly extrinsic value criteria, usually of a cultural, historical, or personal nature.

13 "By claiming to be intrinsic to the nature of literature, it [aesthetic criticism] implies that the nature of literature is aesthetic. But, in fact, literature has no inherent essence, aesthetic or otherwise. It is an arbitrary classification of linguistic works which do not exhibit common distinctive traits, and which cannot be defined as an Aristotelian species. . . . The idea of literature is not an essentialistic idea, and no critical approach can, without distortion, make essentialistic claims upon literature" (Hirsch, p. 135). Critics who hold such an essentialistic view of literature are usually very firmly bound to aesthetic categories and frequently feel uncomfortable with texts whose interpretive meaning is didactic. I am thinking here in particular, within the context of Canadian fiction, of the awkwardness of so much commentary on such writers as Hugh Hood, Morley Callaghan, and Hugh MacLennan whose fiction obviously has didactic purposes.

14 Hirsch writes, ". . . an interpreter, like any other person, falls under that basic moral imperative of speech, which is to respect an author's intention. That is why, in ethical terms, original [as opposed to non-authorial] meaning is 'the best meaning'" (p. 92). Hence Hirsch's "fundamental ethical maxim for interpretation": *"Unless there is a powerful overriding value in disregarding an author's intention (i.e., original meaning), we who interpret as a vocation should not disregard it"* (p. 90).

15 "Mandatory Subversive Manifesto: Canadian Criticism vs. Literary Criticism," Introduction to *Minus Canadian: Penultimate Essays on Literature (Studies in Canadian Literature*, 2 [Summer, 1977], 137-45).

[16] "Romance and Realism in Western Canadian Fiction," in *Another Time* (Erin, Ont.: Porcépic, 1977), p. 58.

[17] See Robert Kroetsch, "Contemporary Standards in the Canadian Novel," in this book.

On another occasion, I would take the time to argue that the writer invents culture in a socio-political sense as well as in an Arnoldian and in an artistic or aesthetic sense and that the critic extends, by his elaboration on the writer's text, these cultural worlds on behalf of the writer.

[18] "The Politics of Self-Parody," in *The Performing Self: Compositions and Decompositions in the Languages of Contemporary Life* (New York. Oxford Univ. Press, 1971), p. 29

[19] See Kroetsch, "Contemporary Standards," in this book.

Incidentally, in terms of my capacious definition of fiction, invoking the criterion of national consciousness, one could argue that George Grant's *Lament for a Nation: The Defeat of Canadian Nationalism* (Toronto: McClelland and Stewart, 1965) is one of our most important pieces of fiction.

[20] See Robert Kroetsch and Diane Bessai, "Death is a Happy Ending: A dialogue in thirteen parts," in *Figures in A Ground: Canadian Essays on Modern Literature Collected in Honour of Sheila Watson*, ed. Diane Bessai and David Jackel (Saskatoon: Western Producer Prairie, 1978), p. 208.

WILLIAM H. NEW

When I began to consider what I was going to say this morning, I thought about the implications of the word "standards," and I confronted what seemed to be an endless series of boxes inside boxes inside boxes . . . . Robert Kroetsch has explained evocatively why this is so, and my words are not a gloss upon his paper, but simply footnotes to his exploration of the language of understanding.

You can see the set of boxes I had in mind if I say that the word "standards" implies an effort to distinguish: but to distinguish what? To distinguish quality, obviously — but *quality* of what? Quality of craft? Quality of mind? Quality of vitality? Quality of judgement — which involves ethical and moral dimensions? Now obviously, all of these are related, and, all in all, they talk about the quality of the imagination, of an aesthetic (though not necessarily moral) vision. But how do we talk about it? How do we probe the implications of the quality of the imagination, both for the writer and for the critic? It doesn't seem to me that it is my business as a critic necessarily to tell a writer how to write, but rather to record another fiction, to record the nature of *a* reader's reaction, and therefore to comment on the relation between the critical process and the book, the essay, the poem.

If I can step sideways for a moment, and talk about one of my experiences as editor of *Canadian Literature*, I think I can lead us back into this notion of standards. *Canadian Literature*, as you know, publishes poetry as well as criticism. As you might guess, a lot is submitted to this periodical and not all of it can be accepted. One of the things that has fascinated me is the degree to which Canadian unity forms the subject of so much unsolicited verse. My problem: as a committed citizen, I applaud the subject; as editor and critic, I have rejected almost all the verse that came in. Why? Because it was not good enough. (Here is the issue that we are facing today in connection with fiction: *"Good," how?*) The verse was ethically respectable. For me, it was politically approvable. The craft was often competent, as far as it went, but often it went only as far as rudimentary mechanics: subjects and verbs agreed, the metre was regular. The craft was respectable, but in many of the works, not purposeful, or not made purposeful. Hence it was at war with the intended subject, and created a different meaning. For meaning lies in method. In these cases, vocabulary, associations of rhyme, the effort of the act of achieving regularity all undercut the subjects.

Now, if the creative act involves mastery of craft, which in turn involves recognition of the manner by which meaning happens, then the critical act involves a certain agility of response, a genuine sympathy for craft, and an adeptness at elucidating the meaning that is lodged in form. Agility, sympathy, adeptness — these words, too, have their implications and return me to the initial notion of standards, for tied up in the critical response is the question of the legitimacy of any particular reaction. If we assert the primacy of moral standards or political standards in judgement, then we have an obligation to know what we mean. Are we asking literature to reflect society, communicate the values in society, communicate the valuelessness in society, reform society, alter society, ruin society? Or is there no connection with society at all? Is art merely artefact, or is art only art when there is a reader? By themselves, these seem abstruse notions. But they nonetheless colour literature, colour the way we react to such matters as explicit sexuality in literature, blasphemies in literature, violence, human degradation, revolutionary thought, extreme conservative thought in literature. We must, therefore, pay these notions some attention.

We often distinguish between that which is gratuitous and that which is functional in literature. But if we ask that literature espouse values, that it aspire to demonstrate the humane possibilities of the human condition, we can be charged with sentimentalizing human experience, with denying blindly the ugliness too many

35

people live with. And if we assert the "realism" of ugliness and violence, we can be charged equally with romanticizing, celebrating anti-values for whatever reason, perhaps just to be thought aesthetically eccentric.

Now it is easy to see that many theorists create containers within which to work. The Christian critic has a container or limiting frame of reference. So does the Marxist critic. So does the Freudian critic. So does the Jungian critic. So does the Structuralist critic. Such containers provide a language of interpretation that often reaches further into a given work than might be possible without a committed position, but it also establishes limitations. Bound with the containing vision are expectations that literature serves or must serve a particular function, that literature must be susceptible to a particular pattern of response. I regard myself as an eclectic critic, out of a quite deliberate refusal to accept preliminary definition of the kind of critical process in which I should be involved or of the kind of result I will get. The important thing is to respond to the writing. But it would be too easy to make the next jump of regarding this critical stance as in some way morally superior. It is easy to say that the committed critic is committed to a cause. Often less easy to see, but in many ways far more important to recognize, is the fact that the eclectic critic can be committed to a cause without knowing it, and further, that this undeciphered commitment will affect both artistic and critical standards, will colour the kind of critical fiction he or she constructs.

There are, therefore, several questions we have to ask. For example, will our evaluation be inflated if a work hints at a value we approve of, or deflated if we oppose the moral stance of the work? Will moral, ethical, national, political concerns matter more to us than the question of craft, the inventiveness of language, the power of invention lodged in language? Will we make a satisfactory distinction between popular literature which determinedly provides escape from the present without challenging the reader's security, and other literature, equally open to being popular, which refashions the reader's own creative capacity to see and understand people? Will we recognize and admit the degree to which an education in and experience of our own society shape our criticism? Will we realize that the degree to which we share cultural values and make communal assumptions about acceptable and unacceptable behaviour moulds even our manner of appreciating experience? I claim there is a strong relation between literature and society, but I

36

reject definitions that impose preconceived limits upon artistic creation, or critical possibility, or evaluative judgement. Nationality is not a criterion of literary worth, but a cultural accoutrement of a writer or reader, an *ambiance* in which one acts. The writer and reader should both be aware of how it affects one's writing and reading, but it should never be defined so as to become a necessary ingredient in art, an obligation defining the artist, an ingredient which, if missing, would deny the value of the art. We have to understand the limitations of rigid standards and of imported standards. We are asked at this gathering to name the "best" hundred Canadian novelists. When facing the question of whether any single forum or any single ballot could adequately set up a canon of anything, we have to remember to distinguish among the different kinds of questions we can ask, the kinds of questions I have been alluding to, for they lead to different judgements. If we do not preserve our own flexibility, we lose some of our imaginative freedom. And, if we lose our imaginative freedom, we lose our capacity both for creating and for appreciating art.

WARREN TALLMAN

The conference brochure says: "The final result will be the identi-
fication of those novels which have established themselves as
Canadian classics." "Novels," I thought. "Canadian," I thought.
"Classics," I thought. And thinking of contemporary authors in
Canada, I dreamed a dream.

And there was General Washington upon a slappin' stallion,
A-givin' orders to his men, I guess there were a million.

"Only a million," I thought. And the dream shifted. There
was General Washington, tall in the saddle, on the southern bank
of the Potomac River, or was it the Trenton, hurling a newly mint-
ed American dollar *in a northerly direction*. Thankfully for Canada
in the North, this object fell to earth into the centre of New York
City and began to form into Continental Flying Object. This Continental Flying Object, CFO, was in the form of a triangle: on one
side there was Space, bulging it out; another angle was Time,
speeded up; the third angle was Population, enough on the Atlantic
Seaboard in those days to get Continental Flying Object into the
air. In the middle was General Washington's dollar, the money
principle, the black hole.

For a time Continental Flying Object, barely lifted into the
air, circled around over the Seaboard where the Population was.
Not until approximately 1850 could it veer out westward with
Population force to enact the Money as energy principle. Now at
approximately 1850 a different object was forming, an Author-
ship, in contention with Continental Flying Object and its New
York Money control towers. This Author-ship was first manned by
our dear old captain, Ralph Waldo, not to mention Nathaniel,
Henry David, Emily, Edgar, Herman, and Walt. 1850: the liberated authors. Liberated, because they were the first to create works
which could not possibly have been written in England or Old
Europe. They wrote from this continent.

Continental Flying Object and Author-ship began to move
west. But before Continental Flying Object moved west, it established a literary power base in New York City called The Publishers, who contend with the Author-ship by mass producing literary

38

hamburgers with outlets: scandal-burgers, crime-burgers, history-burgers, book-of-the-month-burgers, celebrity-burgers, sports-burgers, sex-burgers, review-burgers, movie-burgers, money-burgers, therapy-burgers, religion-burgers, food-burgers, fad-burgers, fashion-burgers, home-burgers, construction-burgers, and, for those with more delicate tastes, soufflé-burgers à la *New Yorker*, à la New York wit, à la New York polish, shine, and style. Because these burgers had everything to do with Money, they became a guide mechanism of Continental Flying Object, and in direct contention with the liberated authors and their Author-ship.

But as Continental Flying Object veered off west in the 1850s ("there's gold in them thar hills!"), the Author-ship kept pace. Under its influence, the liberated authors gave way to the eccentric authors. *In fifty little years the eccentrics began to appear.* From Idaho, mad Ezra Pound, from Oakland, mad Gertrude Stein, from New Jersey, mad William Carlos Williams, and from the Mid-West, mad Theodore Dreiser (his mother saw angels dancing around the bed when he was born) and Vachel Lindsay:

> beat an empty barrel with the handle of a broom,
> hard as you are able, boom! boom! boom!

Just as the Continental Flying Object was concentric, the Money principle in the middle gathered all together in a oneness and sold it with all possible alacrity at the highest possible price. The Author-ship stayed firmly eccentric (let it all out and let's see what the hell is happening on this continent), and, because they wanted to know, the eccentric authors became even more eccentric: looney Ernest Hemingway (clowns and movie-stars were his speed), loonstock Fitzgerald (with a small boy's notion of what it would be like to be rich), looney Sherwood Anderson (he created a small town), looney Morley Callaghan (he created a small town in Toronto), looney William Faulkner and his dream — southern comfort.

Just as Continental Flying Object made it out to California in the West in the 1850s, so in the same 1950s did the Author-ship. But after the liberated and the eccentric authors. In the 1950s in California, in the West, the authors felt free, free of New York hamburgerland publishing, free to write for one another, hoping that someone would look over their shoulders, free to write any which way, who's to say, and thus keep their tickets on the Author-ship. Duncan with his rhetorical accumulations: "I have seen the evil in

Johnson's eyes." Allen Ginsberg with his clown-show performance: "Forget your underwear, we're free!" Jack Spicer, listening for Galahad. Michael McClure talking with lions. Ed Dorn, with a gunslinger at his side: "Yi Yi, The cowboy's eyes are blue, the top of the sky is too." And Robert Creeley: "People, people, people, people, America, when will you give this country back to the people?" And many another one.

Continental Flying Object kept pace, black hole in the middle. But this same 1950-time, that Author-ship arrived at California in the West, it also arrived at Canada in the North. The same freedom, but with a difference: Continental Flying Object trying to invade Canada in the North has had its problems. Thankfully, Population sinks in the scale, Space increases, the Time factor goes wonky, and the Money in the middle declines. Continental Flying Object lurches, loses force. So the Author-ship sails free.

The Author-ship sails free, I dream, free of Continental Flying Object, free of New York, free of novel, free of poem, free of drama, free of critiques, free, and this freedom is my standard for contemporary authorship here in Canada on the North. Here the significant authors feel free, free to use new forms, free to use old forms. Continental Flying Object has overwhelmed the United States on the South, threatens to overwhelm California on the West, but has not yet overwhelmed Canada on the North. And just as well, for the Author-ship is a vessel of life, the Continental Flying Object, a ship of death.

This is for Robert Kroetsch, knowing that lilacs will soon again bloom in the dooryard, and the Mackenzie River once again begin to flow.

DISCUSSION

The discussion for this opening session of the conference began with a plea for the suspension of aesthetic judgements until such time as the foundation for these had been properly laid by a thorough exploration of Canadian cultural and intellectual history, particularly of the nineteenth century, and by an incisive examination of the assumptions of our criticism. Such preparation is necessary, it was asserted, because there is a continuum, however unacknowledged at present, of which contemporary Canadian writers are a part.

The novelist Sylvia Fraser also opposed the judging process, which she denigrated as dispassionate and disinterested, but she did so because she felt that it produced an atmosphere of "artist as criminal."

The question of artistic freedom, thus introduced, was then taken up by several speakers. Warren Tallman felt that one of the great virtues of Canadian writers and the Canadian writing scene in general is that freedom does prevail: that Canadian writers can publish easily, that they do not worry about the volume of publication, and that they therefore can proceed to write first, for themselves; secondly, for their friends; and lastly, for anyone else. Tallman's optimism was, however, challenged by others such as Gerald Noonan, who queried the degree of authorial independence from the environment and the audience, and by Douglas Gibson of Macmillan, who closed out the discussion by propounding the publisher's view in the following reflections:

> If the author, the novelist, acts in an entirely free manner and ignores the audience, then he or she is not going to sell any copy. Publishers are always faced with the grave problem of weighing commerce and art. We can always publish the truly excellent, knowing that in time our judgement will be vindicated. But obviously we cannot go on publishing only the truly artful which is ahead of its time. We're immensely proud of having published Jack Hodgins' *The Invention of the World*, which has been mentioned here in praiseworthy terms already, but we've lost a lot of money doing that. In time, perhaps in ten to fifteen years, we'll make money on it. But the public will respond to formula fiction à la Arthur Hailey with enthusiasm, and the booksellers follow.
>
> The harsh economic realities are that a first novel in Canada does damned well if it sells 2000 copies. To price a book successfully (which means in competition with a price established in New York based on cheaper printing and a larger print run), we have to print at least 5000 copies. Now, it doesn't take a mathematical genius to see that a good sale of 2000 copies and a print run of 5000 copies don't harmonize. What do you do? You usually end up sucking up your guts and

printing up 3000 copies, and underpricing a book which should sell at $15.00 by putting it on the market at $10.95. And even then, people balk at the price.

In other words, I'd like to be Mr. Gloomy Businessman at this conference. A publisher, I suppose, is in the Shavian position of a boy among men, or a man among boys. In the commercial world he's regarded as hopelessly literary and idealistic; in the critical and literary world he's regarded as a crass Scrooge. I suppose that's something we have to live with.

SESSION TWO: Thursday Afternoon, February 16, 1978

Ronald Sutherland: The Two Cultures in the Canadian Novel
Panel
Naïm Kattan
Elspeth Cameron
Antoine Sirois
Yves Thériault
Discussion

The Two Cultures in the Canadian Novel

RONALD SUTHERLAND

The topic chosen for this panel, ladies and gentlemen, is a timely one indeed, now that the cultural schizophrenia of Canadians is threatening to reach a terminal stage. Since it cannot be treated in purely technical literary terms, divorced from social, psychological, and political implications, the subject is a delicate one, likely to be charged with emotional overtones. Nevertheless, it is more than appropriate at this particular moment in Canadian history and could prove to be rich in insight, for novelists are often the best diagnosticians of a society's ills. I will admit right away that I cannot pretend to be an entirely objective, scientific analyst — like many Canadian writers, I am myself involved emotionally. And having lived and worked most of my life in a French-speaking milieu, while at the same time maintaining close contact with English-speaking Canada, I cannot take the position of Raymond Souster's three-line poem dedicated to Gaston Miron. Called "Tragedy," it reads as follows:

> After the hand-shake
> "Je ne parle pas anglais"
> "Je ne parle pas français"[1]

In fact, being emotionally involved, I find myself of late sometimes depressed by various turns of events — the obscene, racist remarks at the National Unity Task Force meeting in Winnipeg, the pontifical utterances of Camille Laurin and Pierre Trudeau. I keep thinking of a story told by American historian Avery Craven at the beginning of his book *The Coming of the Civil War*. Two Confederate soldiers are retreating after Lee's surrender at Appomattox. Both are wounded, tired, hungry, completely demoralized. After walking several miles in silence, one turns to the other and says: "Damn me if I ever love another country."

On the other hand — if you will permit me to be personal a moment longer — I see positive aspects to the current turmoil. I speak for a fairly large segment of the Canadian population which is frequently ignored, those whose families are mixed. I have one English-speaking sister, nine half-sisters and brothers who speak no English at all and who as a singing group were considered reputable exponents of the folksong tradition of Quebec. I have a nephew on the Calgary police force, an aunt in a Roman Catholic convent, a great uncle who was a Protestant clergyman, one cousin who teaches French, and another cousin who left Quebec because he could never learn to speak it. Yet the family, as my wife, who has to make the meals when we all get together, will tell you, is remarkably close. And I can say right now that I do not see either my family or the country falling apart. The strains we are experiencing today I see as labour pains — the periodic turning-in upon ourselves as the contractions, the resounding calls for Unity, *Souveraineté, Association*, or what have you — as the deep breathing, and even the occasional cursing as a natural result of stress. It will be a difficult birth, no doubt — after a gestation period of well over a century, that is to be expected. And quite likely it will be a multiple birth, possibly even quintuplets, as several commentators, including most recently the former editor of *Le Devoir*, Claude Ryan, have suggested. Which would be fitting, perhaps, for Canada has a certain reputation for surviving quintuplets. But whatever the case, I am convinced that it will be the creation of a new family, a new nation, a new concept of nationhood, with the components this time starting out on a basis of shared experience and acknowledged equality.

The shared experiences, of course, are the key to the subject of "The Two Cultures in the Canadian Novel." Since the novel is by its nature a reflection of individual and collective psychology, as well as of society and social values, the co-existence of two major linguistic groups in Canada has naturally had an effect upon Canadian novel writing. For our immediate purposes, this effect may be divided into four general categories. The first category is "Examination of English-French Relations," as for example in Hugh MacLennan's *Two Solitudes* and *Return of the Sphinx*, Philippe Aubert de Gaspé's *Les Anciens Canadiens*, Rosanna Leprohon's *Antoinette de Mirecourt*, James De Mille's *A Comedy of Terrors*, François-Benjamin Singer's *Souvenirs d'un exilé canadien*, Robert de Roquebrune's *Les Habits rouges*, Lionel Groulx's *L'Appel de la race* and *Au Cap Blomidon*, Robert Fontaine's *The Happy Time*, Roch Carrier's *La Guerre, Yes Sir!*, James Bacque's *Big Lonely*, Jacques Godbout's *Le Couteau sur la table*, Claude Jasmin's *Ethel et le terroriste*, and my own novels *Lark des Neiges* and *Where Do the MacDonalds Bury Their Dead?*

The second category is "Image of the French-Canadian in English-Canadian Novels and Vice Versa." I am thinking here of books where the actual relations between the groups are not explored to any significant degree, but which do contain characters from both language communities. Examples are Hugh Garner's *Storm Below* and *Silence on the Shore*, William Allister's *A Handful of Rice*, Rex Desmarchais's *La Chesnaie*, Roger Lemelin's novels, Patrice Lacombe's *La Terre paternelle*, André Langevin's *L'Elan d'amérique*, Jean Simard's *Les Sentiers de la nuit*, Antonine Maillet's *Les Cordes-de-bois*, Mordecai Richler's *The Apprenticeship of Duddy Kravitz*, Adrien Thério's *La Colère du père*, Earle Birney's *Turvey: A Military Picaresque*, Anne Hébert's *Kamouraska*, Gwethalyn Graham's *Earth and High Heaven*, Morley Callaghan's *The Loved and the Lost*, Margaret Laurence's *The Diviners*, Gérard Bessette's *La Bagarre*, and others, as the auctioneers say, too numerous to mention.

The third category is "The Bilingual Character in Canadian Novels," and here I mean works which attempt to analyze the social and psychological implications of bilingualism. All the novels of the first category of necessity have bilingual characters, as do several of the works in the second category. But the question of what being a bilingual individual in Canada actually signifies — the advantages and disadvantages, the heightened consciousness, the traumas, the fractured identity, and the broadened perspectives — this question, curiously enough, is examined in very few Canadian novels. Among them are MacLennan's *Two Solitudes* and *Return of the Sphinx*, de Roquebrune's *Les Habits rouges*, Groulx's

L'Appel de la race and *Au Cap Blomidon*, Desmarchais's *La Chesnaie*, and my own two novels mentioned earlier.

The fourth and final category is "Symbolic Representation," which includes those works which seem to deal with the Canadian situation indirectly through symbols or allegory. Dave Godfrey's *The New Ancestors* is an example, as are, to my mind, Yves Thériault's *Aaron*, Hugh Hood's *You Cant Get There From Here*, and Hubert Aquin's novels. There may be others with which I am not familiar.

These, then, are the four general categories pertaining to the "two cultures" in the Canadian novel — French-English Relations, Respective Images, the Bilingual Character, and Symbolic Representations. Before looking more closely at any of these categories, however, I would like to clarify what I understand by the "two cultures."

Commentaries, books, laments, celebrations, white papers from government gurus — the subject of culture has come in for a great deal of attention in Canada recently. And, in a statement which is being repeated in Quebec to the point of becoming a cliché, the latest instance in an article from The Canadian Press by novelist Victor-Lévy Beaulieu, is that in contrast to English Canada, which has none of its own and is "odorless, colorless and tasteless," Quebec has a distinctive culture. In other words, instead of talking about the "two cultures" today, we should really be discussing culture and the absence of culture in the Canadian novel.

Now what exactly is distinctive about Quebec culture, and how is it that anglophone Canadians can stumble through life either in a state of cultural nudity or in hand-me-downs from a prosperous uncle? According to famed ethnologist Konrad Lorenz, who ought to know what he is talking about, a culture is a system of social norms and rites which are "emotionally felt to be values."[2] In the sociological sense, therefore, culture is simply the way a group of people lives and what these people live for. It is what they are attached to emotionally, and as Lorenz further points out, there is always a strong tendency for this emotional attachment to lead to a conviction of superiority. Or as Hugh MacLennan aptly phrased the idea in *Two Solitudes*, identification of "the familiar with the excellent."[3]

Unfortunately, the emotional factor in culture can often have a blinding effect, so that comparisons become irrational if not absurd. Mackenzie King, as everyone knows, made important decisions only after consultation with the Great Beyond, through his mother, his dog, and various others among the deceased — a practice, incidentally, which would likely have proven a real challenge for even the sophisticated eavesdropping techniques of the R.C.M.P. But King's recently published journals reveal everything, and in them there is a telling remark. It seems that the ghost of Sir Wilfred Laurier appeared to him one night. Then King adds that he was not sure whether to believe that spectre or not, because, after all, Laurier was a French Canadian! The grave may be a fine and private place, but even there, for those with convictions of group superiority, the cultures do not embrace.

Beaulieu's recent remarks are happily restricted to the living, but still they read as if he were announcing, "My wife is beautiful and everyone else's is not." Camille Laurin, Quebec's Minister for Cultural Development, not wanting to be so positive that people might question the urgent Québécois need for a guardian and mentor such as himself, might rather declare, "My wife is more beautiful than anyone else's, but her performance will not attain an acceptable norm until she has had expert counselling." And René Lévesque, operating on a wavelength of his own, has complicated the issue by speculating that the women of Quebec, like those of New York after the blackout, have been performing so well since the election of his Parti Québécois that there is now a mini baby-boom in the province.

But to get back to what is distinctive about Quebec culture, a number of observations can be made — and by someone, let me make absolutely clear, who knows it and still loves it well. For one thing, the people of Quebec eat more McDonald's hamburgers than any other group in the world. We have apparently taken a significant bite out of the 35 billion — or is it 40 billion now? — all washed down with millions of gallons of Pepsi and Coke. We are also high on the list for what is known as Poulet frit à la Kentucky, and we certainly cannot be accused of lagging behind, the unions willing, in construction of Holiday Inns and pizza parlours. We warn our good buddies about "un Kodak avec un qui va prendre ton portrait" on our CB radios, so far still clean and green with *l'Office de la langue française*; and we wept for Elvis. Since like everyone else we get them to look at the pictures rather than to read, the language barrier is no impediment to our buying our fair share of *Playboy*, *Playgirl*, and *Penthouse*, as well as their French-language imitations. And let me tell you, the *National Enquirer*

48

pales into a Sunday school tract beside some of Quebec's yellow journals.

The fact of the matter, to put it bluntly, is that contemporary Quebec culture is probably more American than the cultures of other regions of Canada. What does the average Québécois want? A bungalow in the suburbs, colour television, a two-car garage big enough for standard Chevs or Fords, and a butterball turkey in the microwave oven. He also shares the primordial Canadian winter dream of palm trees and sun-drenched beaches, accounting for the annual southward migration (some 300,000 last Christmas alone!) of hundreds of thousands of Québécois, and explaining, I might add, how a Quebec novel came to have the title *O Miami Miami Miami*. The author of this novel? None other than Victor-Lévy Beaulieu.

Ironically, then, while certain Quebec commentators claim that there is no difference between Americans and English Canadians and that English Canada has no culture of its own, it is the Québécois who seem to have become more completely Americanized. Because of obvious superficial similarities, English Canadians, especially of late, have tended to resist American influences as best they could. Québécois, on the other hand, because the language difference provides an illusion of security, have not felt the same need to resist. In New England alone, there are between two and three million people of French-Canadian descent — the contacts and the affinities have existed for a century and a half.

This is not to say, however, that there is nothing culturally distinctive about Quebec. The point is simply that when a custodian of Quebec culture makes the same remark about English Canada, he is talking through his tuque. What is truly distinctive about both Quebec and the various other regions of the country is the way in which we have all managed to retain a little individuality in face of the overwhelming allurements of the American way of life. Mind you, I do not believe that there is anything inherently wrong with copying the Americans; although it does seem that both Québécois and English Canadians are perversely determined to imitate all the errors and shoddy, more questionable practices of the United States, such as the Madison-Avenue, "Big Sell," no-holds-barred promotion of a book recently attempted by a Toronto publishing house, rather than to emulate the many admirable American achievements. Still, in spite of everything, the various regions of Canada have retained some distinctiveness. We have all come up with blends, to be sure, and in much the same manner. But then every living culture is a blend, constantly revitalizing itself, giving and taking, adapting to new realities, interrelating with other cultures. Canadians, like everyone else, operate at different cultural levels — the intimate-family level, the larger circle-of-acquaintances level, one or more regional levels, the national level, the North American level, and in some cases the world-community level. At the regional level, Quebec certainly has its distinguishing features, but so do the other regions of Canada. And since we are all in the same boat, trying to preserve and nurture what distinctiveness we have, we would do well to recognize sentimental attachments for what they are and to suppress the all-too-human inclination to confuse them with criteria of superiority.

Having said all this, I am now obliged to admit that the expression "the two cultures of Canada" is misleading. At the national level, there is the single culture which all Canadians, like it or not, share, resulting from the history, the crises, the climate, the sports events, the conflicts, the political institutions, and everything else we have experienced together. At the more immediate and poignant regional level, there are numerous cultures in Canada, and they are not defined by provincial boundaries. The Gaspé, l'Acadie, Vancouver Island, Westmount, Cape Breton Island, the Kingdom of the Saguenay, Southern Ontario, for example — each has a measure of cultural distinctiveness. The global term "two cultures of Canada," therefore, is inexact. To be precise we should be saying "the two major language groups of Canada." And this is not the only semantic problem these days. Many anglophones, it would appear, are disturbed by the expression *deux nations du Canada*, interpreting it to mean "two nations of the nation." But in international French usage, the word *nation* really signifies "ethnic group," while English "nation" more closely corresponds to the word *état*. In Quebec French usage, however, the word *nation* has apparently come to mean both "ethnic group" and "language group." In the expression *deux nations*, one of the *nations* is the Québécois ethnic group, while the other is the language group composed of all those, whatever their ethnic affiliations, who are English-speaking.

In view of the current semantic permissiveness, then, perhaps we may be excused for the expression "two cultures." For practical purposes it does have a certain usefulness, for I believe that it is generally understood to pertain to the specific interrelationship between anglophones and francophones of Canada, irrespective of regional differences in culture. That, in any event, is my own interpretation.

To return at last to the four categories of novels related to the two cultures, those under the first heading, "English-French Relations," may be further characterized according to tone. In most cases it is not difficult to tell whether the author looks upon *rapprochement* between the language groups positively or negatively. Groulx's *L'Appel de la race*, for example, unequivocally takes the position that contact between English-speaking and French-speaking Canadians is inevitably to the detriment of the latter, and that intermarriage actually leads to degeneration, possibly even madness, or at least to what the author calls "cerebral disorder." Which is not a comforting thought when one thinks of how our future may be in the hands of such prominent political figures as Pierre-Elliott Trudeau, Claude Ryan, Robert Burns, and Pierre-Marc Johnson. Rex Desmarchais's *La Chesnaie*, despite its strong nationalistic flavour, is much more positive than Groulx's novel. One francophone character even speaks of giving a "rayon d'honneur" in his library to the great works of English novelists and goes on to state that "Les Anglais avec qui il s'était trouvé en relations avaient montré de la bienveillance et de la largeur de vue"[4] — The English with whom he had had dealings had shown goodwill and broadmindedness. Another character, English-speaking, adopts a similar attitude toward the French and feels that "Les deux races du Canada doivent s'unir"[5] — The two groups in Canada must unite. Hugh MacLennan's Paul Tallard, in *Two Solitudes*, is, of course, a symbol of the union of the two language groups, and there can be no doubt about the author's attitude toward *rapprochement*. MacLennan sees Paul as the ideal Canadian, moving easily between the two cultures and embodying both. Yet it is important to note that Paul's role as an archetype presupposes the continuing existence of two unilingual communities. MacLennan does not seem to be projecting a nation of Pauls, but rather a nation of separate identities intermeshed and made viable by a sufficient number of Pauls.

One thing all the books of the first category have in common is recognition that the co-existence of two language groups in Canada has created tension and conflict. Most of the novels focus on particularly troubled historical periods: Aubert de Gaspé's *Les Anciens Canadiens* examines the Conquest; de Roquebrune's *Les*

Habits rouges examines the Rebellion of 1837; Groulx's *L'Appel de la race* examines the dispute over Bill 17 and the teaching of French in Ontario; MacLennan's *Two Solitudes* examines World War One; Carrier's *La Guerre, Yes Sir!*, and my *Lark des Neiges* and *Where Do the MacDonalds Bury Their Dead?* all partly examine the strained relations caused by World War Two, MacLennan's *Return of the Sphinx*, Godbout's *Le Couteau sur la table*, Bacque's *Big Lonely*, and Jasmin's *Ethel et le terroriste* examine the violence of the 1960s.

More important than the description, however, is the light these novels throw upon the causes for tension and conflict between English- and French-speaking Canadians. In general one can say that the combatants are presented as victims, of circumstances such as actual warfare over which they have no control, of deeply ingrained prejudices or loyalties passed down to them, or of pseudo-scientific theories of race. Desmarchais and Groulx, for instance, incorporate into their works certain nineteenth-century racist hypotheses which are now discredited. Particularly bizarre is the position taken by both authors that language and physical appearance are somehow interdependent. Says one of the characters in *La Chesnaie*: "Comme vous je suis d'avis que les Canadiens français doivent conserver leur physionomie française"[6] — Like you I think that French Canadians have to keep their French looks. Groulx's novel expounds at length on what are called "Saxon traits," and one can only presume that to the author all anglophones looked alike.

It must be pointed out, however, that Groulx and Desmarchais, like a number of other Quebec authors and many contemporary Quebec leaders, were conditioned by fear, the fear of assimilation and of loss of identity. Last year a book was published called *Bilingual Today, French Tomorrow*, by retired Lieutenant-Commander J. V. Andrew. It is an ignorant, sadly ridiculous book — the author even sees French take-over plots in the naming of car models "Acadian" and "Parisienne." The argument of the book, that among other things Toronto, Vancouver, Halifax, and Calgary are in imminent danger of becoming French-speaking, is, of course, a virtuoso performance in inanity. Yet apparently thousands of Canadians have bought the book — it is in at least a sixth printing; I should be so lucky to see any of my eight books to date reach a sixth printing — and who knows how many have been persuaded by Andrew's invitation to fear? Now obviously Andrew has simply reversed the position of authors such as Groulx and Desmarchais, but with a significant difference — Andrew's fear is absurd, that of the French Canadians was entirely justified. For many years the French language was, in fact, threatened in Quebec, not to mention elsewhere in Canada. I must say, however, that the current exercise in the politics of fear by some political leaders in Quebec is not similarly justifiable. Outside of the Island of Montreal, only six point two per cent of the population of Quebec are anglophone, and of this remnant some forty per cent are bilingual, compared to eighteen per cent bilingual francophones. In other words, without benefit of government decree, Quebec has been steadily becoming solidly French. More rapidly outside Montreal than within, to be sure, but Montreal, which draws much of its workforce from outside the metropolitan area, has been slowly following the same pattern.

There is probably no need for me to dwell on the inculcated prejudices and loyalties which authors of the first category see as causes for conflict between Canada's two major language groups. Religion was a large factor, as seen especially in the works of Groulx and MacLennan. I might note that my own novels, which are quite explicit with regard to acquired prejudices, are based on realities I experienced growing up in the East End of Montreal. Personally I place much of the blame on the separate school systems of Quebec — the supposed imparters of wisdom, school teachers, were often the evangelists of hate. Some, unfortunately, still are.

One last observation can be made about the books which examine French-English relations. As MacLennan states and the other authors imply, Québécois see themselves as a collectivity, while English Canadians tend to see themselves as individuals. This divergence is still creating problems, the current language-of-education debate in Quebec being a case in point. The government would appear to be willing to sacrifice individual rights in the presumed interests of the collectivity, while anglophone Quebeckers, with absolutely no representation in the P.Q. Government, are constantly, sometimes even hysterically protesting about the erosion of individual rights. Interestingly enough, however, the very dispute is having the effect of modifying the traditional postures outlined in the novels. Many English-speaking Quebeckers, feeling beleaguered, are forming a circle like the musk oxen of the North, thinking of themselves increasingly as a collectivity; while a significant number of Québécois, having noted that many of the P.Q. leaders are fluently bilingual and send their children to private schools with excellent English courses, are thinking of themselves as individuals about to be shafted for a collective higher cause, creating an every-man-for-himself situation. Somehow, somewhere, there has to be a mutually acceptable middle ground, and I think the present confrontation is herding both groups toward it. As my old grandmother, who brought nine daughters to this country in 1907 on a tramp steamer from Scotland, fighting off hungry rats and lusty sailors all the way, used to intone, "It's an ill wind that blaws naebody guid."

The other three categories of novels pertaining to the two cultures can be examined more briefly than the first. So far as "Respective Images" are concerned, suffice it to say that they range from stereotypes, such as the cartoonist Gagnon in Callaghan's *The Loved and the Lost*, Frenchy Turgeon in Garner's *Storm Below*, a whole Westmount family in Simard's *Les Sentiers de la nuit*; then the merely nominal, such as Yvette in Richler's *The Apprenticeship of Duddy Kravitz*, the boss Stevens in Bessette's *La Bagarre* or MacFarlane in Maillet's *Les Cordes-de-bois*; to fully developed, intriguing characters such as Doctor Nelson in Hébert's *Kamouraska* and Jules Tonnerre in Laurence's *The Diviners*.

"Symbolic Representations" lend themselves to many different interpretations which transcend our present purposes and are really the subject of a separate study, but the "Bilingual Character" category raises a number of questions which are quite pertinent. Actually, a student at l'Université de Sherbrooke, Henri Leperlier, has just completed under my direction an M.A. thesis on the subject. Leperlier, who comes from France, was rather surprised to find a marked dichotomy of attitudes toward bilingualism in Canada. De Roquebrune's *Les Habits rouges* is one of the earliest novels to explore the psychology and social problems of the bilingual Canadian, through a character who is a Québécois and an officer in the Army during the suppression of les Patriotes. The setting is thus ideal to illustrate how being bilingual can both enrich and diminish the quality of life, by broadening perspectives and opportunities while at the same time engendering the painful dilemma of opposing allegiances. The heroine of my novel *Lark des Neiges*, Suzanne MacDonald, experiences the same duality in the later context of the Conscription Crisis and the Separatist confrontations of the 1960s, and she reaches the point where she actually wishes that she had never learned two languages. The fact of the matter, as all novels in this category exemplify, is that being bilingual in Canada could be far more complicated than simply having the capacity to speak both English and French. There were economic, social, psychological, and historical factors to be considered. For a long time in Quebec, English was identified with economic power and social ascendency. Thus, for the anglophone to learn French meant no more than acquiring a second language, but for the francophone to learn English meant the possibility of losing a mother tongue, or re-enacting the Conquest, and of betraying his heritage. Moreover, to climb in the business world right in Quebec, the francophone was humiliatingly obliged to learn English; the anglophone could choose to remain blissfully unilingual from womb to tomb and still be President of Sun Life. Hugh MacLennan's Huntley McQueen, Sir Rupert Ironsides, and all the others from St. James Street are hardly figments of his imagination — they are based on clearsighted observation. That was definitely the way it was. As my character Suzanne MacDonald learns, even in factories in the East End of Montreal, promotion from worker to foreman was dependent on a knowledge of English, except where the foremen and other bosses were imported directly from Britain, in which case there was no possibility of promotion at all.

Here again, however, the real-life situation is rapidly changing in Quebec. Executives are going to Berlitz, those who have not decided to go to Toronto. Thousands of English-speaking children are now taking immersion French courses in school. The new era began with the Quiet Revolution of the 1960s, which had a profound psychological effect recorded in the more recent novels. It broke the grip of the old classical colleges and provided post-secondary education free to the working classes. It brought Quebec into the twentieth century and applied the coup de grâce to the old inferiority complex. The Québécois working man will no longer tolerate being ineligible for the job of foreman, and that, ladies and gentlemen, is in essence what is rocking the boat in the formerly "belle" province.

Things have surely changed. Even the storied "solitudes" are not what they used to be. The careers section of the old garrison newspaper, the *Montreal Star*, featured many announcements in French before it folded, and what with the Prime Minister, provincial premiers, various other political figures, union leaders, the Task Force, journalists, writers, and professors all traipsing back and forth across the country, it must be difficult for the average Canadian who can read and turn on a television set to remain totally unaware of what is happening in the nerve centres of the nation. And even if he does not always grasp exactly what, he at least knows that something is happening, and that it could profoundly affect his life.

In fact, however, the "solitudes" were probably never quite as forbidding and formidable as Canadians have been led to believe, or perhaps even like to believe. We have discussed a few of the novelists who broke the language-and-culture barrier. In the world of literature there are many others — translators, anthologists, poets, critics, playwrights, literary historians like Lorne Pierce, Camille Roy, B. K. Sandwell, people of unrestricted vision such as my good friends here today, Yves Thériault and Antoine Sirois, Naïm Kattan and Elspeth Cameron. A forthcoming double biography, *Annie Howells and Achille Fréchette*,[7] by James Doyle, provides another, truly fascinating example, and a fitting way, perhaps, to conclude this address.

Achille Fréchette met and married Annie Howells in Quebec City, where her father was serving as American consul. Since he worked in the Translation Department of the Federal Government, the couple settled in Ottawa and remained there for thirty-three years, from 1877 to 1910. Annie was quite a well-known freelance journalist in the United States, and she also had a modest reputation as a fiction writer. Achille Fréchette was a published poet of some renown. But what makes their story fascinating is that Annie was the sister of the prominent American novelist and *Atlantic Monthly* editor William Dean Howells, while Achille was the younger brother of the French-Canadian poet equally prominent in his own right, Louis-Honoré Fréchette. And on both sides the families were tight-knit.

Add to the scenario the fact that post-confederation Ottawa was a fermenting mass of political, religious, and literary energies, in all aspects of which the Fréchettes were involved, and the import of Doyle's book becomes obvious. Annie and Achille eventually came to run a kind of literary salon. Among their friends and guests were Octave Crémazie, Duncan Campbell Scott, Pamphile Lemay, Wilfred Campbell, James Le Moine, Archibald Lampman, Alfred Garneau, Sara Jeanette Duncan, Pauline Johnson, a variety of American writers, and Sir Wilfrid Laurier, who came to dinner with William Dean Howells. Within the group there was much mutual aid in terms of contacts and publishing opportunities. The youngest Fréchette brother, Edmond, for instance, had his stories of the Canadian West published through a friend of Annie's.

Of particular interest is the background Doyle's book provides to the old and continuing debate in Quebec between the reformist, pro-republicans and the isolationists, and to the bitter "Separate Schools" dispute, in which Achille as a school commissioner was deeply engaged. Quebec's Quiet Revolution was a long time brewing, it seems. Efforts to reform the school system by introducing more scientific and vocational training began a full century before the Lesage Government finally shook free from the ecclesiastical stranglehold.

The biography also explains how Louis Fréchette came to translate Howells' novel *A Chance Encounter*, and it solves the mystery of the English and French versions of Fréchette's *A Christmas in French Canada* — Louis Fréchette wrote both versions himself, with his sister-in-law Annie polishing up the English text.

A rather intriguing commentary on the difference between American and Canadian nationalistic spirit emerges from Annie Fréchette's comparison of John A. MacDonald's funeral with that of Abraham Lincoln. "Of course the military and different societies were out," she wrote in a letter to her sister, "still there was all the quiet and decorum of a private burial — not a flag or a banner to be seen along the whole line."[8] Annie's dealings with Mrs. Theodore Coleman, a writer for the strongly imperialist Toronto newspaper, the *Mail and Empire*, are revealing. Both Annie and her brother were dismayed by the English-Canadian trait, at the time, of servile allegiance to Great Britain. They would, I trust, have been heartened by the new Canada of the 1980s.

Like the novelists who have tackled the delicate and difficult theme of English-French relations, Annie and Achille did something to bring English-speaking and French-speaking people together, to increase mutual understanding, and to penetrate the so-called "solitudes." As Doyle's biography makes clear, however, at the same time as they lived closely together for more than half a century until Achille's death in 1927, each marriage partner had a private and separate world, a personal career to follow in a different mother tongue. And it occurs to me that we Canadians of both major language groups have been misinterpreting Rilke's famous poem given national currency by MacLennan's classic novel. The Rilke lines which MacLennan actually quoted are:

Love consists in this,
that two solitudes protect,
and touch, and greet each other.

Like Annie Howells and Achille Fréchette, perhaps we should stop
worrying about the perfectly natural, often enough necessary solitudes, and concentrate a little more on the protecting, the touching,
and the greeting.

NOTES

1 Raymond Souster, "Tragedy," in *The Colour of the Times* (Toronto:
  Ryerson, 1964), p. 105.
2 Konrad Lorenz, *On Aggression* (London: Methuen, 1966), p. 236.
3 Hugh MacLennan, *Two Solitudes* (Toronto: Macmillan, 1957), p. 75.
4 Rex Desmarchais, *La Chesnaie* (Montréal: L'Arbre, 1942), p. 146.
5 Desmarchais, p. 180.
6 Desmarchais, p. 178.
7 Since published by the University of Toronto Press (see note 8).
8 James Doyle, *Annie Howells and Achille Fréchette* (Toronto: Univ. of
  Toronto Press, 1979), p. 95.

NAÏM KATTAN

I was very impressed by the ideas that Ronald Sutherland expressed
in his paper. I'm always very delighted to participate with him in
discussions on themes on which we agree basically. Our views sometimes go different ways, but are still complementary to each other.
Maybe if Jacques Godbout were here, he would dispute certain of
Professor Sutherland's ideas, which would have made it more interesting for those of you who were expecting that. I won't be able
to do that, because I just can't play a role — I agree with him.

So I would like just to go on in the discussion he has opened,
to add certain themes. The first aspect I would like to mention is
one that is very well, radically, and sometimes violently expressed
in Scott Symons' novel, *Place d'Armes*. Symons, who came to
Montreal from Toronto knowing French, not only speaking it but
writing it, has an idea which I think is very basic (even if he does

sometimes express it in a quite violent way): the two peoples, the founders of the country, have come with *bagage*, a certain kind of wealth or heritage that they brought with them from their countries of origin, France and Britain. When we look at the novels that have been written by them since, we can see that this attitude to the countries of origin is quite basic, at least in the earlier novels, and that the way to deal with time in Canada by the novelist, was a way to deal with memory. In western Europe the way to deal with time was to go to the first written book, which was the Bible. I was reading an article yesterday by a French writer who said that it was very important to note that the first printed book in western Europe was the Bible, that the first narrative, the first *récit*, that was printed in the West, was this basic book for the Christians, Jews, and Moslems (the Koran is partly an adaptation of the Bible). This memory, based on the will of God, has been transmitted to Canada and accepted by it. The two founding European peoples wanted to be faithful and loyal to this memory. Although they were divergent in methodology, they were both Christian: Protestants and Catholics. The basic element was there: there was God, and there was Christ, and there was Judaism behind. The memory then belonged to France and to England. It became divergent later on. For Robert de Roquebrune and Catharine Parr Traill, the way to deal with this immediate past was nostalgia and a prolongation. An English Canadian was not cut off from England; he was still living in a dominion; he was still part of England. Whereas the French Canadian was cut off from France; cut off first by the Conquest, and also by the French Revolution, because it was felt that disloyalty to the Bible and to God was portrayed by a lot of the new masters of France. There were elements in French-Canadian writing and thought which accepted the Revolution, but I am just opening things for discussion.

The other theme which I think is very relevant in the discussion of the novels of the two languages is the attitude towards power. Language itself is power, is at first the oral way of mastering or describing our world. Power is involved as well in the change from oral to written language. But when we go to the social structure of the country, then we find there are elements of what Sutherland did mention in his paper, which are also divergent; the power is accepted by both languages, if we take Lionel Groulx, or Sinclair Ross, or anybody. It is mostly accepted in the nineteenth century or at the beginning of the twentieth that the power was God's power (this is basic in Groulx's writing). But when we go from the rural area to the industrial area, we then see the feeling that the birth of industry and commerce was effected by English-speaking Canadians (some of them were immigrants who accepted English). They were seen as the people who were disrupting the rural space, but they were also establishing a new kind of power. Many French-Canadian novels, from Gabrielle Roy's *Bonheur d'Occasion* to those of Yves Thériault and André Langevin, felt that this power of establishing an industrial state and financial power escaped the French Canadian. They felt very often that the power of money and the power of industry was detrimental to the soul, and that the real power was still the power of God. In the French-Canadian novel, a feeling of having a mission in the new land was replaced first by a feeling of deprivation, and then by a feeling of deprivation combined with a feeling of revolutionary quest.

Another important element in the relationship of the two languages is the relationship to space. Jacques Cartier was the first to say this is the land of Cain — again, a biblical idea. It was felt that there was an element which was very hard in the new land, but what is important in that (and this is prevalent in most of the novels of French and English Canada) is that, in contradiction to the United States, there was respect of the land and respect of the law in the land. In Canada there was the mountie rather than the cowboy, a respect for a law theme rather than an outlaw theme. But also prevalent in all North American settlement is the theme of change, of ephemerality. You are always on the move, going west, going east, going north, or south. While in Europe, France, England, Russia, etc., the peasant settled in an eternal land, in North America the land was always new. But it also belonged to memory and to God, because it was established by people coming from Europe, so that this idea of settling the land by respecting it, and by always being on the move, creates another kind of relationship to space in the city as well as in the rural areas. Again, I'm only opening the discussion; I won't pursue it more.

The term "two cultures" is both conceptually accurate, as Ronald Sutherland implied, and a misnomer. As Robert Kroetsch pointed out this morning, we are all creators of our own fictions, and the notion of two cultures originates with Hugh MacLennan's phrase "two solitudes," itself suggestive of the somewhat unpleasant value systems of Upper and Lower Canada. Incorporated into our collective imaginations, mythologized, this phrase has moulded our view of Canada — life does imitate art. A dramatic example of the writer as inventor of the world, Hugh MacLennan can be seen as a Canadian Adam who, in the process of naming, has influenced for better or worse the way we perceive this country. To name, as all writers and all parents know, is to assume a godlike power; it imposes an order on the flux of real experience which may or may not correspond to the inherent qualities and characteristics of the person, political movement, art form, etc., named. A name, in short, is an overlay or veneer, and, as such, can distort. In Robertson Davies' play *Overlaid*, which is named for this phenomenon, the force of puritanical goodness is symbolized by a granite tombstone; its deadly weight holds down a buoyant vitality and imagination. Indeed, many of Davies' fictional characters rename themselves as they come of age and thereby express something closer to their true selves. This concern for what is really there or here has correctly found critical expression in a seminal article by Robert Kroetsch which appeared in the *Journal of Canadian Fiction*, called "Unhiding the Hidden: Recent Canadian Fiction,"[1] in which he explored briefly the *un*-naming, *un*-covering, *un*-hiding, both personal and national, which to his mind typifies contemporary Canadian fiction. For a nation overlaid, first as a colony of England, then as an economic satellite of the U.S., this concept is central.

On close examination, the concept of two cultures in Canada, though it may sound right, even feel right, is a distortion. Even an attentive reading of *Two Solitudes* would indicate, as Sutherland points out, that French and English are not so much divided, as parallel, analogous cultures, throwing forward characters on both sides who are troubled by their growth into individuality despite those forces greater than themselves which threaten to overlay the self-expression they seek. (I think, by the way, this explains why so many such novels are set in periods of unrest or in difficult times — their settings emphasize the nature of forces greater than the individual.) The true solitude in this novel is the loneliness in the heart of each character, French or English, as he or she takes stock of his society and its people.

If we look at Quebec as a region, as Mari Stainsby does in "Paraphrase of the Vision: French-Canadian Writing in Translation,"[2] we see at least three main groups of writers, three cultures in fact: French, English, and Jewish. The main distinctions that can be drawn between these groups are founded on styles and structures which are consequent upon cultural and linguistic common backgrounds: for example, the liturgical rhythms common to the Jewish writers, and their tendency to a messianic vision. But a comparison of Leonard Cohen, Mordecai Richler, and Jacques Godbout would probably result in setting Cohen and Godbout together vis à vis Richler. The point, and it is one made elsewhere by Sutherland in *Second Image: Comparative Studies in Quebec/Canadian Literature* and *The New Hero: Essays in Quebec/Canadian Literature*, is that the general *ambiance* Willam New spoke of this morning prevails. Cultural modes prove ultimately to be superficial compared to both the wider environmental context and the deeper, intimate, personal vision. In contemporary French-Canadian fiction, we see the struggle of the individual to throw off an overlay — frequently depicted as English-Canadian domination to be sure — in favour of individual expression; "unhiding the hidden," a reality that was there all along. As Quebec's motto suggests, "Je me souviens." Or, as Saint-Denys Garneau once wrote, in a carefully argued discussion of nationalism in literature, "the whole task, I think, the whole problem consists in freeing the human spirit, not in freeing French-Canadians."[3]

This task has been taken up by English writers as diverse as Margaret Atwood, Marian Engel, Robertson Davies, Margaret Laurence, Adele Wiseman, Jane Rule, Scott Symons (and I would agree with Naïm Kattan that Scott Symons is an extremely important writer in this context). A central image for me in this cross-cultural Canadian concern occurs in Margaret Laurence's African short story from *The Tomorrow-Tamer*, "Godwin's Master," in which a dwarf "oracle" is freed from the box he is kept in, only to discover the even greater obstacles he faces in assuming the responsibilities of freedom, self-expression, and self-reliance. As Morag in *The Diviners* says, "I make boxes for myself and then I get furious when I find I'm inside one.''[4] Unhiding the hidden proves to be a similar Titanic struggle. It is always easier simply to say, as does the title of Jane Rule's second novel, *This Is Not for You*, than to live outside the comfortable box of an imposed role. Underneath, the real self is likely, in Margaret Atwood's phrase, to be "a patchwork self,"[5] needing a strong, integrating drive. It is not easy for the voice to hear itself, as Kroetsch commented this morning.

The struggle to hear that voice, and to record it, whether it be French, English, Ukrainian, American, or whatever, seems to be a common concern in Canada. The soul of the nation, like the self Atwood described, is patchwork, fragmented. It is because a number of sub-cultures exist that MacLennan was able to project into the French consciousness after less than ten years in Quebec (and as far as my research reveals at the moment, he only knew three French Canadians personally to any extent, one of whom was a Huguenot);[6] that English Canadians can feel acutely the dilemmas of French characters in French-Canadian novels; that Margaret Laurence can write with astonishing authenticity of the inner lives of Africans during the Ghanaian struggle for independence. Let us not lose sight of the fact that the word "novel" means new, that it implies the freedom, or striving for it, to create anew.

NOTES

[1] Robert Kroetsch, "Unhiding the Hidden: Recent Canadian Fiction," *Journal of Canadian Fiction*, 3, No. 3 (1974), 43-45.
[2] Mari Stainsby, "A Paraphrase of the Vision: French-Canadian Writing in Translation," *British Columbia Library Quarterly*, 26, No. 1 (Jan. 1963), 3-10.
[3] Saint-Denys Garneau, "Notes on Nationalism, 1938: January 30th," in *The Journal of Saint-Denys Garneau*, trans. John Glassco, introd. Gilles Marcotte (Toronto: McClelland and Stewart, 1962), pp. 104-05.
[4] Margaret Laurence, *The Diviners* (Toronto: Bantam, 1975), p. 188.
[5] Margaret Atwood, "Hair Jewellery," in *Dancing Girls* (Toronto: McClelland and Stewart, 1977), p. 114.
[6] Further research revealed that MacLennan derived much of his French-Canadian material for *Two Solitudes* from Ringuet's *Trente Arpents*. For a full discussion, see Chapter vi of my *Hugh MacLennan: A Writer's Life* (Toronto: Univ. of Toronto Press, 1981).

ANTOINE SIROIS

Ronald Sutherland has stated how the two cultures are shown in Canadian novels. Complementing his statement, I would like to see if the novels express values that are part of the cultures concerned, and, if so, which ones they imply, and more specifically, to what extent they represent the values of the groups. Culture, implying a way of being, a way of thinking, the way a large group behaves, is more or less a common denominator, but it may comprehend some values that can be different in one sub-group or another, in one social stratum or another. Literature is a social, cultural product and, therefore, is much influenced by the society that breeds it. It expresses social transformations, whatever may be the story told, the setting, or the forms. A system of values underlies the whole work and can be specific to novels of such and such a period. In fact, I do find a number of values specific to each group. I even find a certain number common to both literatures for definite periods.

If I consider the idyllic novels, or most of the *romans du terroir* in both languages up to World War II, novels generally concerned with land and nature, I detect a common attachment to the rural area seen as the Garden of Eden, the same interests in the pioneer life, the farmers rooted in the land, the people living in small communities, nostalgia for the world of peace and protection. Quite a few values are at stake in these novels, often written by city dwellers: security, well-being, independence, physical and moral health, fraternity. I also find in these novels a common reprobation of the city considered as the land of evil, be it Toronto, Montreal, or even Calgary. The city is morally and physically dangerous.

If I turn from idealized and moralizing novels written in an agrarian era to more realistic ones appearing after World War II, when the characters dare to venture into the cities, what values are at stake? I do find again, in the novels of both languages, values proper to one group or even common to both. Whether it be Hugh MacLennan, Morley Callaghan, Leonard Cohen, Mordecai Richler, or again Jean Simard, Gérard Bessette, Gabrielle Roy, or Françoise Loranger, a new interest is taken in urban social problems. The new bourgeois establishment with its craving for money, prestige, and power comes under severe attacks. The new material and superficial ambitions of the city conquerors, like Jean Lévesque or Duddy Kravitz, are ridiculed. On the other hand, many heroes, having rejected values of the past, suffering from isolation, start on the personal quest for new moral and intellectual values, particularly, social justice and fraternity.

By the '60s, the not-so-Quiet Revolution in Quebec arises, and, with it, the need for personal commitment in the search for collective identity. The novels now express frustration, anguish, or violence, not only in their content, but also in their language and form. There is a similar tension and anger, a similar search for a collective identity, a cultural nationalism, maybe in a less dramatic way in English-Canadian writing a few years later, and a new inventiveness of language and form.

After this very brief panorama of values belonging to each of the literatures concerned, and even often common to both, may I now ask to what extent these novels represent the cultures they are rooted in? If we still consider literature as a social-cultural product, novels still express a milieu, a group, but do they not express the values of a very specific group? Are these novels the image of a whole culture, or do they only represent values of a small part of it, namely the élite or the intelligentsia? Should we find in the novels the image of Quebec or of English Canada, or is rather what we discover the vision of the writer's social group? In no way do I deny the importance of that vision — good writers give expression to sets of ideas which so far have remained unexpressed. This conference states that one of its objectives is to provide a norm which can serve as a curriculum of reference to teachers of Canadian literature. Therefore, we should ask whether we are not often tempted to present the novels as an expression of English Canada or of French Canada as a whole, while they might articulate the views of very specific groups, the groups of those who write the stories, not necessarily of those who are written about — farmers or labourers, or whatever they are. To view our novels as the representative expressions of our cultures is to demand, it seems to me, that we are sufficiently grounded in the social histories and the existing ideologies of the cultures we are dealing with.

I have a very close friend in Quebec. I shall have the courage to name him because I think that the occasional newscast has revealed him to you — his name is René Lévesque. When I was invited to come here, I asked him, "Do you advise me to go into a foreign enemy country?" He said, "Yes . . . yes, I think they won't hurt you too much." And then I said, "Well, don't do anything stupid while I'm there." So he goes to Ottawa, to the Prime Minister's Conference, and he walks out of it. I watch him on my television in my motel room and I say to myself, "What has he done to me?"

My viewpoint is going to be very brief, and it's going to be quite different. Because I left school in the eighth grade at age fifteen and never went back, I cannot think or reason as an academic would. I respect the academic viewpoint, but I cannot express it. I'm a journeyman writer; I've written a lot; I write to earn my living. I write in Quebec; I write in French. I could write in English; I possess the language sufficiently for that; I have, in fact, written in English. I found at one point, however, that, in spite of my command of English, whenever I went to Toronto, I was still foreign to whatever was happening there. This was not deliberate; it did not stem from hatred, but from ignorance, from indifference. Having discovered this, I wrote in French for my Quebec, and I became deliberately a solitary. I became someone confined to his own Quebec, which was accepting him and making possible the continuation of his career as a writer, as a storyteller. At no point did I feel that I should extend my communication to the rest of Canada. Through translations I became known in certain parts of Canada, even considered as a writer in certain universities, but this was not deliberate on my part.

I am not saying these things in an attempt to hurt anglophones. I'm saying them in order to explain why French-Canadian literature has been so parochial, a literature totally identifying with Quebec, with only occasionally a novel or certain characters within a novel having some preoccupation with two solitudes or two cultures. We have not been given to recognizing the existence of the rest of Canada. That was wrong, I admit. But I think that circumstances, and the attitude of the rest of Canada, prompted our disregard.

Images of family and generation dominated the discussion for the conference's second session.

David Jeffrey initiated the pattern with the observation that surrounding the language differences of Canadian literature is an obsession in both major literary communities with families and family history, and a fascination with the Bible as an "elemental cultural document . . . a literature that lies behind our literature." To instance both from Canadian custom rather than literature, he pointed out that, whereas in Europe it was traditional to place a family registry at the beginning or at the end of the Bible, in Canada (and subsequently in the United States) the family registry was customarily placed in the middle, significantly sandwiched between the closing words of the Old Testament: "And he shall turn the hearts of the fathers to the children, and the children to the fathers lest I come and smite the earth with a curse," and the opening words of the New Testament: "These are the generations of Jesus Christ." Jeffrey wondered about the significance for Canadian literature of this conjunction of family history and biblical centrality.

Naïm Kattan responded that the idea of employing the Bible as historical document is basically Middle Eastern, and that history was conceived of in this practice as being not merely a series of events, but a manner of relating to the eternal. This relationship, according to Kattan, and this is something he has outlined in his book *La mémoire et la promesse*, is dominated by such central metaphors as movement (God telling Abraham, Jacob, Ishmael to go elsewhere) and promise (the promised land). He also reminded the audience that the significance of other biblical patterns in Canadian literature have been explored by D. G. Jones in *Butterfly on Rock: A Study of Themes and Images in Canadian Literature.*

In reply to a lament that the West still feels culturally colonized in the Canadian context, Ronald Sutherland evoked Margaret Laurence, Rudy Wiebe, Sinclair Ross, Ethel Wilson, and Earle Birney to contend that the real pattern of cultural colonization in Canada now might very well be West to East, rather than the other way around. Sutherland then developed the notion that culture is a matter of layers, as suggested by Elspeth Cameron, and that the fundamental layer is that of the family, added to but never displaced by other culture layers such as that of province, region, and nation. Cameron went on herself to elaborate on this point by suggesting that problems within the family unit, especially of self-expression, are often employed by Canadian writers as paradigms of national or international issues.

John Moss's assertion that it is good in a family to acknowledge differences and that therefore we should acknowledge that "Quebec literature is a French-language literature" and "Canadian literature is an English-language literature" was quickly countered by Sutherland and Yves Thériault. Sutherland protested that the differences are individual or regional, and suggested that the differences between F. P. Grove and Leonard Cohen are much more dramatic and culturally distinctive than those between Jacques Godbout and Cohen. Thériault also insisted that the regional differences are most important and that these do not preclude one's being a *Canadian* writer, whatever the language one writes in.

In response to a query concerning the present relationship of French-Canadian literature to the culture of France, Kattan suggested that there were three ways of settling in the new land: the new beginning by willful rebellion of the Americans, the continuation of contact with the mother culture by the English Canadians, and the reluctant separation from the mother culture through conquest of the French-Canadians. This latter produced, he pointed out, nostalgia for and an idealization of France, but these have now been largely replaced by the feeling of contemporary French-Canadian writers that they are different from the writers of France; and France in its turn frequently registers a similar feeling of difference by treating French-Canadian writers as exotic, or by referring to them as Americans who write in French. Thériault confirmed this latter point by stating that American influences in French-Canadian writing are much more pronounced than French influences.

Kattan, however, was challenged by a suggestion that the separation from the mother culture was just as critical an individual cultural experience for English-Canadian writers as for French-Canadian writers (an assertion which Kattan did not accept) and by the suggestion that settlement and immigration patterns in Canada made cultural distinctions a function of generational differences and of an East-West division in experience. Kattan remarked that this latter point too would have to be qualified, since the movement west has always been a part of French-Canadian literary consciousness, as exemplified by Philippe-Antoine Savard and others, and that the Western experience is, therefore, part of a national continuum and is not autonomously regional. Sutherland added that many of the dimensions of East-West movement in our literature have been explored by W. H. New in *Articulating West: Essays on Purpose and Form in Modern Canadian Literature.*

The panelists were then asked to predict the future direction of the Canadian novel. Sutherland, John Moss, and Antoine Sirois opined that Canadian writers would become more individualistic and more experimental, while Kattan predicted that they would reflect the growing contacts between the two major cultures, and Cameron concluded that the period of national navel-gazing has ended, that Canadian writers would take for granted their audience's familiarity with their settings, and that while this could lead to individual experimentation, it might also lead to the addressing of broad, international issues. Thériault ended the discussion on a personal note with the hope that his newest novel would take the right direction with the public, he hoped, "with a translation in New York."

SESSION THREE: Friday Morning, February 17, 1978

W. J. Keith: The Thematic Approach to Canadian Fiction
Panel
Henry Kreisel
D. G. Jones
Laurie Ricou
John Moss
Discussion

The Thematic Approach to Canadian Fiction

W. J. KEITH

Perhaps I can best indicate my basic response to this subject by describing the circumstances under which I come to be speaking here. When I first received Ernest Ingles' invitation to deliver a lecture on "Themes in Canadian Fiction," my first reaction was, I confess, one of amusement — amusement because, "if small things we may with great compare," reasonable equivalents might be to ask René Lévesque to address you on the benefits of federalism or (more to the point here) Mordecai Richler to discourse on the novelistic virtues of Frederick Philip Grove. Not long before, in my capacity as editor of the *University of Toronto Quarterly*, I had, in self-defence and with something approaching desperation, penned a statement on editorial policy that insisted: "The Journal does not normally print thematically oriented criticism." And only a week or so before, while setting essay topics in my undergraduate course on Canadian fiction, I had appended (as, nowadays, I invariably do) the following instructions: "You are expected in each case to concentrate on the novels *as works of art*; it is not sufficient merely to compare and contrast themes."

So I contacted Ernest Ingles, thanked him for asking me, but explained my difficulty. Thematic criticism, I said, was my *bête noire*; if I began to talk about "Themes in Canadian Fiction," I would inevitably end by arguing that the thematic approach was in fact the least promising way of coming to terms with Canadian fiction (or any other). Imagine my surprise when he replied: "Most interesting. Why don't you come and do just that?" So here I am, unable to resist the opportunity of speaking on this extremely important subject to a captive audience (or reasonably so — I understand that the exit-doors remain unlocked). I wish to thank the organizers of the conference for being flexible enough to accommodate my position and for allowing me to substitute a different, if related, title. Nonetheless, they decided — very properly — to appoint a panel on which thematic critics are strongly represented. All in all, this promises to be quite a spirited session.

I

Exact definitions of literary terms always bother me, so my first action upon acceptance was to look up "theme" and "thematic criticism" in any literary reference-books that lay to hand. M. H. Abrams, in his *A Glossary of Literary Terms*, referred me from "theme" to "motif" and there I found the following:

> A motif is sometimes called a theme, but the word "theme" is more usefully employed to denote the thesis or doctrine of a didactic work. . . In modern criticism, the word "theme" is often used also to signify the abstract concept which is said to be embodied in the structure and imagery of a nondidactic or purely imaginative work.

"Said to be" implies scepticism, and the definition goes on to question the usefulness of the term outside explicitly didactic works. And when I looked up "Criticism, Types of" in W. F. Thrall, A. Hibbard, and C. H. Holman's *A Handbook to Literature*, I discovered that, although they listed no less than eight types (impressionistic, historical, textual, formal, judicial, analytical, moral, mythic), "thematic criticism" was not included. (They admit that "there are certainly others," but imply that these are relatively unimportant.) I quote these definitions because the results may well come as a surprise to those familiar with the habitual procedures of Canadian literary criticism, in which, presumably because of the influence of Northrop Frye, the emphasis has (especially in the last two decades or so) been predominantly thematic.

I am tempted to say exclusively so. One has only to assemble titles of the most influential essays or volumes for the thematic bias to become evident. They consist either of dominant images suggestive of grand generalization to which literary experience — so it is argued — significantly conforms ("Wolf in the Snow," *The Bush Garden: Essays on the Canadian Imagination, Butterfly on Rock: A Study of Themes and Images in Canadian Literature, The Haunted Wilderness. The Gothic and Grotesque in Canadian Fiction*) or directly advertise the themes to be extracted from literature (*Survival: A Thematic Guide to Canadian Literature, Patterns of Isolation in English-Canadian Fiction, Sex and Violence in the Canadian Novel: The Ancestral Present*). Even individual issues of the journal *Canadian Literature* are, more often than not, arranged along thematic lines. All this being so, it was hardly surprising that, when the organizing committee of this conference came to plan topics for these sessions, "Themes in Canadian Fiction" should, as a response to an almost Pavlovian preconditioned stimulus, inevitably spring to mind. We are, frankly, obsessed with thematics. Indeed, where (one asks with some unease) can we turn for a literary-critical account, not of the subject-matter of Canadian fiction, but of Canadian fiction itself? Sad to say (and publishers, please note) the answer is: nowhere.

This matter has been troubling me for some time. I know many individuals similarly dissatisfied with the current emphasis, but, until recently, challenges to the literary-critical *status quo* rarely appeared in print. I have detected, however, ripples of discontent in the last few years, and at least one four-square confrontation of the problem. I refer to Frank Davey's hard-hitting article, "Surviving the Paraphrase," which appeared in *Canadian Literature* in the issue for Autumn 1976. My own opinion is that Davey begins excellently and presents a number of searching criticisms that desperately needed to be voiced. I would like now to summarize his analysis of the situation and then to explain why I differ from him in his positive recommendations.

Davey's position is contained in the following series of highly selective extracts:

In its brief lifetime, Canadian criticism has acquired a history of being reluctant to focus on the literary work — to deal with matters of form, language, style, structure, and consciousness as these arise from the work as a unique construct. It has seldom had enough confidence in the work of Canadian writers to do what the criticism of other national literatures has done: explain and illuminate the work on its own terms, without recourse to any cultural rationalizations or apologies.[1]

Davey complains that the thematic critic's role "is not to attend to language, form, or even to individual works of literature, but to something called by Jones in *Butterfly on Rock* 'our imaginative life,' by Moss in his *Patterns of Isolation* the 'national being,' and by Frye in *The Bush Garden* 'cultural history.' " Davey calls these approaches "extra-literary" and "at worst, anti-literary" because the "focus of such criticism invariably rests outside the writing . . . ." The movement, he continues, is towards paraphrase: "The critic extracts for his deliberations the paraphrasable content and throws away the form. He attends to the explicit meaning of the work and neglects whatever content is implicit in its structure, language, or imagery" (p. 6).

I have quoted Davey at length because, up to this point, I agree wholeheartedly, and could not hope to improve upon his crisp and clear-headed account. I agree also with two of his related points: first, that recent Canadian writing "has been engaged for the most part at the level of form and language rather than theme" and so needs a critical approach capable of responding to this challenge (p. 5). (Davey specifies the mature work of Rudy Wiebe here, and, since he wrote, Jack Hodgins has come into prominence and added substance to the argument); second, that thematic criticism tries "to define a national culture but chooses to work with materials — literary themes — that are . . . international in nature" (p. 8). Davey's diagnosis seems to me impeccable — but I have grave reservations about his proposed course of treatment. Moreover, I can locate the parting of our ways at a specific point in the following passage:

The motivations of thematic criticism strike one as essentially defensive in respect to both the culture and the literature. A declared motive has been to avoid evaluative criticism, which

Frye has claimed would reduce Canadian criticism to a "huge debunking project." An even more important but undeclared motive appears to have been to avoid treating Canadian writing as serious literature. For there are many kinds of non-evaluative criticism which these critics could have practised other than the thematic. (p. 9)

Why "non-evaluative" — which Davey never questions? The whole of his argument seems to have been moving towards a plea for a more discriminating and so evaluative reassessment. I expected him to say (as I *do* say) that Canadian literature has now attained a sufficient solidity and stature that we can invoke high standards without any fear that the subject might succumb to the process. The plain fact of the matter is that Davey ventures so far and then draws back. "It is extremely important," he argues, "that Canadian critics not forget that there are indeed alternatives to thematic criticism, and that most of these do not involve a return to that *bête noire*, evaluation" (p. 9). And he goes on to list possible critical approaches: historical criticism, analytical criticism, genre criticism, phenomenological criticism, even archetypal criticism. This, I must confess, not only disappoints but depresses me. In my view, Davey here shows himself just as much a victim of the pigeon-holing obsession as the thematic critics whose approach he deplores.

At this point I had better lay my own cards on the table. Admittedly, I first studied English at Cambridge and therefore came under the influence of evaluative criticism at what some might call an impressionable age. I still think that "the words on the page" are the first concern of a literary critic, though I agree that one must be sure that one knows not only what the words mean but what associations attach to them at different literary periods — and words vary, we should remember, not only in different ages but in different countries. But I am above all a critical relativist. I believe that "taste" consists in knowing the appropriate criteria to bring to the individual work. The critic must be firm (you will not find me — *pace* Warren Tallman — trying to prove that "crude" is really "fine"), but he must also be flexible. Obviously, it is no good bringing to *Sunshine Sketches of a Little Town* the same critical approaches that one applies to *Middlemarch*. But one discovers the appropriate criteria by attending in each case to the language and its associated qualities: tone, imagery, rhythm, point of view, authorial attitude — not to mention those larger, vaguer entities like form and structure. One will go astray if one starts extracting thematic plums, like Little Jack Horner. Indeed, if one *does* confine oneself to themes (provincialism, political corruption, religious cant, financial intrigue), *Sunshine Sketches* and *Middlemarch* may well appear to resemble each other — but in so doing one will only succeed in distorting and belittling the art of both.

However, I do not wish to be misunderstood. I am not advocating a total neglect of subject-matter and theme. If one ignores what a work of art is about, one soon enters the realm of "art for art's sake," and any attempt wholly to separate art from life leads either to triviality or to absurdity. I am merely insisting that identification of theme is no more than a tentative first step towards mature literary-critical discussion. Again, some authors clearly invite a greater thematic concern than others. Hugh MacLennan is an obvious instance, though I had better state my conviction that *The Watch That Ends the Night* is far and away MacLennan's finest novel, not because its theme is any more important or appealing (let alone "Canadian") than the others, but because of all his novels it is the most satisfactorily realized as art. By the same token, I do *not* consider *The Diviners* Margaret Laurence's best novel — or anywhere close to her best — though I grant that it is thematically the most comprehensive. But artistic and thematic criteria are by no means identical — and ultimately it is the artistic that endure.

Yet here I encounter a difficulty. I have a number of points I wish to make (for example, how can one possibly separate the theme of, say, *As for Me and My House* from the artistry that Ross displays in telling the story?), but when articulated they sound so simple and obvious that I wonder if I am not merely offering platitudinous truisms. Surely, it might be asked, everybody believes all this? Unfortunately, everybody does not. It *ought* to be generally accepted that classifying works of art by subject-matter, without any attention paid to comparative quality, is a waste of time. Yet we find David Arnason, in his collection of *Nineteenth Century Canadian Stories*, trying to resurrect a feeble tale by Rosanna Leprohon (no, "resurrect" is the wrong word: how can one resurrect something that has never lived?) with the comment: "Like Maupassant's later story 'The Necklace,' it tells of lost jewellery . . . ."[2] Only in a critical tradition dominated by pigeon-holing in terms of theme and subject would such a remark pass muster.

And it *ought* to be self-evident that in critical analysis theme can never be divorced from treatment. But, in his little book on Morley Callaghan, Victor Hoar does precisely that. He begins as if he had made a great critical discovery: "Whenever Morley Callaghan has commented upon his apprenticeship as a writer of fiction, he has expressed as much interest in the matter of technique as he has in the matter of theme."[3] But he misses Callaghan's point and so divides his book, simplistically, into two parts: I, The Technique, II, The Themes. I cite these two instances, trivial in themselves, not merely because they are elementary — though they show with painful obviousness the literary-critical inertia that has to be challenged — but because they come from books specifically designed for the edification of students. As it is, they can only teach students bad critical habits. Surely, as critics, we can do better than that?

II

My own objections to thematic criticism are twofold: first, emphasis on themes and related structural patterns generally reveals comparisons rather than contrasts, and often confuses a novel's weaknesses with its strengths; second, the neglect of language is often reflected in linguistic inadequacy within the thematic critic's own prose, and this in turn leads to distortion and crudity of effect. I would like now to pursue these two points in greater detail.

Because he is in no way remarkable for stylistic subtlety, Frederick Philip Grove is a novelist peculiarly suited to the thematic approach. His main thematic preoccupations are easily listed: the pioneering theme; the conflict between generations; the clash between a man's duty to the land and his duty to his wife and family; the inexorable pressure of Time; the contrast between "vision" and reality, etc. But in listing these, and illustrating their recurrence in the novels, one has said little or nothing about the distinctive quality of Grove as a novelist. On the contrary, one emphasizes what the novels have in common but neglects what gives them variety. For Grove hardly ever repeats himself. Niels Lindstedt and Len Sterner are both young and sexually naïve idealists but in strikingly different ways; the general pattern of Abe Spalding's life may resemble that of John Elliot, Senior, but the details — Abe's attempt to dominate the land by machinery against Elliot's reliance on traditional methods, for example — vary considerably. Indeed, although the organic unity of Grove's total *oeuvre* is important, the variety of intention and effect from book to book is even more so. Whatever principles and laws Grove may recognize as operating on earth, he always presents them in particular instances as they affect particular human lives. His emphasis in his novels is invariably on *people*, people who share certain basic attitudes but differ subtly in motive and response, and this concern for individual uniqueness is what sets him off from many so-called "Prairie novelists" who attempt no more than a straight, documentary presentation of the Prairie itself.

If we merely classify his themes instead of examining the ways in which they are transformed into art, we shall fail to do justice to Grove's originality. Moreover, I believe that, if the thematic approach is pursued, some of his best effects will be neglected and some of his weaknesses mistaken for strengths. About two years ago, I remember hearing a "Radio College" program in which *Settlers of the Marsh* was the focus of attention. The commentator concentrated on thematic patterns — Ellen and Clara as opposites, the balancing of scene against scene, the contrasts between rural and urban values, nature and artifice, innocence and experience, etc., etc. All these are, of course, to be found in the book, but the lecturer seemed to assume that they automatically constituted novelistic strengths. Yet it seems to me that the very fact that these patterns are so conspicuous in the novel is, rather, an artistic weakness. The structure is *too* insistent; the content is too readily detachable from the context. *Settlers of the Marsh* has, I believe, many artistic strengths, but these exist despite rather than because of the too-baldly stated themes, the excessively schematic construction.

But I have already expressed my views on the artistry of this novel in print.[4] To demonstrate how Grove creates situations that transcend the thematic, I prefer to turn to a scene in *Our Daily Bread* (a novel, I may say, inexplicably omitted from the conference ballot-list). John Elliot, Senior, is a man who has lived through the pioneering period, and by the time the novel opens has established himself as a farmer in the Saskatchewan short-grass country. We get one memorable glimpse of his pioneering days, and this occurs in a flashback placed strategically in the very centre of the novel. Elliot is on a visit to his daughter Cathleen and his professor son-in-law, Woodrow Ormond, in Winnipeg. They hold a party (as Woodrow explains, "A few guests. . . . Mostly men.

Colleagues of mine, or men in public life"),[5] and Elliot feels uncomfortably out of place in this urban and sophisticated intellectual setting. Suddenly, however, a young man engaged in writing a book on the early history of the West asks Elliot for information about the pioneering period. He begins to reminisce, launches into stories and anecdotes, and gradually the attention of all the guests is centred upon him.

The scene is an extremely complex one, and I can do no more than offer a pale indication of its effectiveness. The main point is that this effectiveness lies not in the pioneering theme itself but in the context that Grove has created for it — a context, moreover, that becomes an inextricable part of the subject. He doesn't have to remind us that eras of historical development (or, to be more accurate, eras of white historical development) were so foreshortened on the Prairies that a single lifetime could span the period from pioneers' sod huts and Red River wagons to cars, sumptuous houses, and maid service at the press of a button. Grove's "meaning" is to be found, not in a detachable theme that can be measured or tabulated, but in the multi-faceted experience of the scene as a whole. In this case the artistry lies, not in language, but in imaginative, creative construction. Here Grove is indisputably a "maker."

But I must now turn to a consideration of language. Thematic criticism, I have said, underestimates the importance of language and style; moreover, thematic critics often demonstrate an insensitivity to language in the way they write about literary works. I detect a vicious circle here. There has been so much ponderous Canadian criticism in the past, dull in more than one sense of the word, that some of our younger critics have rebelled against its standards by writing a direct, forceful, but essentially slangy prose. It is easy to sympathize with their motives, but the fact remains that this is a style in which, to put the matter bluntly, serious literary criticism cannot adequately be written.

Here is a minor example. But first, since I begin by quoting John Moss in a context of disapproval, I should state that Moss is a critic whom I greatly admire when he writes at his best; indeed, I recommend *Patterns of Isolation* to my students as the most useful single book on Canadian fiction. All in all I find Moss (and this is sincerely intended as a compliment) a critic worth disagreeing with. Here, however, I quote a sentence from *Sex and Violence in the Canadian Novel:* "Morley Callaghan, in the 1930s and 1940s, exhibited a fascination with not only the moral but the spiritual implications of violence, but he muted sex somewhat, even in *Such Is My Beloved*, which features two hookers and a priest."[6] Margaret Atwood, in *Survival*, casually refers to "the whores in Callaghan's *Such Is My Beloved*,"[7] and D. G. Jones mentions "the priest's campaign to help two prostitutes."[8] Now Callaghan himself took great care to make the narrative voice in the novel speak not of "prostitutes" or "whores" or "hookers" but of "the girls." In other words, he habitually refers to them, not in terms of their trade, but in terms of their humanity. Ironically, that is part of the central theme of the novel, but it is conveyed through language and thematic critics seem to miss it. In the scene where Father Dowling confronts his bishop we are told that "the way the Bishop said common prostitutes hurt him."[9] To Father Dowling himself they are "the girls" until late in the novel, and on the few occasions when he does refer to them as "streetwalkers" or "prostitutes," he is specifically concerned with their profession rather than themselves. Otherwise it is left to Mrs. Robison, the Bishop, the probation officer — and the critics — to classify them merely according to their commercial and sexual function in society.

I don't want to exaggerate the significance of this example. After all, the girls *are* prostitutes, and Callaghan does not disguise this — quite the contrary, in fact. It is, admittedly, extremely difficult to avoid using such words while discussing the novel, but Callaghan himself was certainly not being puritanically evasive in eschewing the direct terms. To say that the novel "features two hookers and a priest" is to give a misleading impression ("features," with its suggestion of Hollywood movie-advertising, is as much to blame as the reductive "hookers"). A reader unfamiliar with the book receives no clue as to what kind of novel *Such Is My Beloved* really is.[10]

Let me quote a few sentences from the text to bring us closer to the centre of Callaghan's subject and his art:

When Father Dowling saw the girls moved in this way, he was so thankful his whole face beamed with gratitude. He moved his chair closer to the bed. He put his hand lightly and shyly on the little dark girl's head and stroked her hair softly and in him was a joy he had never known before. As he tried to smile at the two girls who had been moved by his presence, he felt more love for them than for any one he had known in his parish, a curious, new love that gave him a strange contentment. (p. 13)

The first thing to notice, surely, is the extraordinary delicacy of this. Callaghan succeeds in being profoundly moving when it would have been so easy to lapse into tasteless vulgarity. He assumes an awareness of modern psychology, but achieves a precision and subtlety that we rarely find in the application of Freudian theories. The novel is, among other things, a study of the relation between *eros* and *agape*, between sexual and spiritual love; this is one of its major themes, but Callaghan embodies it in language that converts it into art, a language that provokes the questioning response but not the crude snigger, We realize that Father Dowling lacks self-knowledge, that he is vulnerably naïve, but we also respect him for his spontaneous goodness, for his genuineness. I am groping awkwardly for adequate words here, but Callaghan made the distinctions and created the essential balance through his words, in the text. And only through attention to Callaghan's words — their tone, rhythm, combinations, and associations — can we come to a proper appreciation of his art. At this level, thematic criticism cannot help us.

III

I have tried to demonstrate, by brief reference to individual details and scenes, how the thematic approach has to be supplemented before anything very useful can be said about a novel as a work of art. With the same overall aim in mind, I would now like to offer a more extended treatment of a single work, and the book I have chosen is Ethel Wilson's *Swamp Angel*. This book seems to me unquestionably a masterpiece; a title that ought to appear on anyone's list of the ten best Canadian novels. I shall start on the level of subject-matter and theme, and then proceed to more directly artistic matters.

Swamp Angel opens, you will remember, with Maggie Vardoe fleeing from her disastrous second marriage, and the main plot focuses upon her gradual development of a new life and a new equilibrium as cook and general assistant in a fishing lodge in the country north of Kamloops. But this plot is punctuated by scenes in Vancouver dominated by Maggie's friend Nell Severance, a wise, obese septuagenarian continually recalling her early life as a circus juggler. We soon realize that Maggie and Nell are being presented as opposites who are yet, in a curious way, complementary. Maggie, trying to escape from a dead past, goes into "the wilderness," the traditional journey for the religious contemplative. Nell Severance, herself a contemplative and in her own words " 'an unusually religious woman,' "[11] remains almost completely indoors (" 'Everything of any importance happens indoors,' " she claims [p. 149], and on the one occasion on which she ventures outside she suffers a fall that has serious consequences); she surrounds herself with a protective screen of cigarette-smoke and harks back to a probably tawdry but in retrospect exotic past. Maggie acts; Nell theorizes. Maggie finds peace only in the wilds; Nell doesn't enjoy (as she puts it) " 'drooling over scenery' " (p. 66). Maggie, then, a swimmer and fisherman who follows the northward-flying birds on migration, is attuned to nature; Nell, still practising her juggling techniques, relies on artifice.

Yet there are some curious similarities. Both have the capacity to help others in distress; both have to find their place in the uncertain country between solitariness and loneliness. Each needs the other: " 'Maggie,' " writes Nell, " 'I miss you very much to talk to and I need humanizing. I'm a bad influence on myself' " (p. 128); and Maggie, in a moment of crisis, thinks: "I wish Nell Severance were here with her acid good sense" (p. 142). If Nell is attached to the Swamp Angel, a revolver that once formed part of her juggling act, Maggie takes with her on her journey "the little yellow [Chinese] bowl which was now her household god" (p. 73). If Nell thinks about religious values, Maggie acts upon them in her day-to-day life — as Desmond Pacey remarked, "Mrs. Severance comes closest to articulating the creed; Maggie Vardoe embodies it."[12]

Although they have been close friends for many years, within the book itself Maggie and Nell meet only once, in a crucial scene in which they discuss the "themes" of the novel. But as soon as we try to list the themes, we find ourselves (or *should* find ourselves, unless we are content with a crude parody) acutely conscious of Ethel Wilson's art as a "maker." So far, my commentary may have suggested a plot as conspicuously polarized as that of *Settlers of the Marsh*, but *Swamp Angel* does not give this impression. The thematic relations between the parts are by no means obvious as we read. Ethel Wilson's art depends to a considerable extent upon her capacity to lead us surely but indirectly towards her unifying "vision."

What, then, are the themes? Well, the nature of marriage, together with the related concern of the individual's place within a larger social unit (often the family unit), is a major one. We do not see Maggie's own marriage (or only the last moments of it), but we see its effects. Nor do we see Nell's marriage, since she has long been a widow, but we see the effects of that too in the attitudes of her daughter Hilda. When Maggie establishes herself at the lodge, we are told that her "union with Three Loon Lake was like a happy marriage" (p. 84), but there she comes in contact, and sometimes conflict, with another marriage, that of the Gunnarsens, trembling in the balance under the strain of the wife's neurotic jealousy and the husband's stubborn obstinacy. There are numerous other references: the happiness of Maggie's first marriage, destroyed by war; Hilda Severance's marriage towards the end of the novel; Vardoe's later liaison with the shadowy Ireen, the eccentric family to which Nell's husband Philip belonged, the humdrum domesticity of a talkative woman who sits next to Maggie on the bus to Kamloops. Moreover, a whole chapter early in the novel is devoted to the Quongs, despite the fact that only the two brothers, Joey and Angus, play any part — and that secondary — in the main plot. But the Quongs are important because they are a true family; they possess a familial loyalty and morale that endures and blossoms despite their relative poverty, cramped living conditions, and apparent cultural deprivation.

It is only after we have been introduced to all these marriages and families that Maggie and Nell discuss the subject — and then Nell, while expressing her faith, "'I believe in marriage'" (p. 150), reveals that Philip was never in fact her legal husband, that they had never married because he did not believe in the "'bonds'" of matrimony, and Nell, the "unusually religious woman," had sacrificed her own principles to his. From time to time, Ethel Wilson allows herself the privilege of authorial intrusion, but the profundity of her treatment of marriage and the family depends almost wholly on the examples fully integrated into the novelistic texture and the "serious irony" of Nell's statement in the context of her own situation. Ethel Wilson's "thought" is of the utmost significance, but it is the thought, not of a philosopher or of a theologian or of a sociologist, but of a creative artist.

Because Maggie has to build a new life out of the ruins of the old, and because this is inevitably a slow process, *Swamp Angel* is also about Time and the relationship between past and present. Here once again Maggie and Nell are similar yet dissimilar; both must come to terms with the past but for different reasons. For Maggie, separation (or, to use the word that Ethel Wilson emphasizes by giving it to Nell as a surname, "severance") is essential in her own interests; the burden of the immediate past has become intolerable, and Maggie must cut all connections. For Nell, however, the past — or, rather, her memory of it — is an indulgence, a sentimentality, an addiction like her chain-smoking. A continual harking back to it can be, like the Swamp Angel itself, beautiful but dangerous. The price of Nell's compulsion is paid by her daughter Hilda in the present. Nell, the wise woman, has sufficient intelligence and courage to cut her links with the past, and she does so, significantly, by sending the Swamp Angel to Maggie for safe keeping and ultimate disposal. After Nell's death, and according to her wishes, Maggie, who has now established the basis for her new life, throws the Swamp Angel into the middle of the lake in which, as a swimmer, she has found a timeless freedom.

If at this point some of you are complaining that my own critique has not yet ventured far beyond thematics and subject-matter, you are quite right. Part of my intention is to demonstrate both the difficulty and the challenge of writing adequate literary criticism about a novel that is at once straightforward and extremely subtle. I have deliberately kept close to the thematic in order to show that even a primarily thematic approach should (must) broaden out if it is at all responsive to the artistry of the work. But, ultimately, this can only be accomplished if the verbal quality is stressed — and so far I have only quoted briefly and in the interests of meaning rather than stylistic effect. Obviously, one could spend a whole lecture and more on detailed verbal analysis. I have time for only the briefest of indicative hints. Most evident (as well as economical) are the *bons mots* of Nell Severance — wise, compassionate, but with a palpable hint of the sardonic:

> [Nell to Edward Vardoe] "You've got a new life ahead" (you poor fool, she thought) . . . . (p. 49)
> [Nell of Edward Vardoe] "He's an unpleasant object but worth salvation I suppose." (p. 49)
> [Nell's creed] "I believe in faith. I believe in God . . . and in man, to some extent at least." (p. 103)

The effect here depends upon the tone of the spoken voice, upon the cadences and pauses that combine to convey a meaning existent only in those same words and that precise order. Any "paraphrase," to borrow Davey's term, destroys the artistic balance. One can draw attention to the effect, praise it, even analyze it, but one cannot recreate it in any other form. The themes can be extracted easily enough, but Nell Severance herself, in all her human intricacy, lives in the words as Ethel Wilson arranges them.

But more subtle and less conspicuous is the effect of Ethel Wilson's own commentary. Take, for instance, the description of Maggie offered through the eyes of Mr. Spencer, the official in the sports shop to which she has gone to sell her fishing flies: "She was not beautiful; she was not plain. Yes, perhaps she was beautiful. She took no pains to be beautiful" (p. 14). Or of Nell Severance trying to save Vardoe:

> She smiled a faint smile but her face was not happy because she saw Edward Vardoe in his helplessness and his meanness and his stupidity and she thought again that life is unfair. "It's not fair . . . not fair," she murmured, and then she went into the kitchen and made a tall pot of cocoa. (p. 49)

There is no "style" here, no "fine writing" — and I have chosen these examples for that reason. What we have is an exquisite sense of clarity, of finding the right sequence of words to convey a meaning: first, Maggie's appearance posed between the plain and the beautiful, a balance established between the polarized words as they are repeated with variations, and all this presented through an observer in the very act of discovery, of responsive assessment; and then the extraordinarily subtle sense of a total situation — Vardoe's inadequacy, Nell's inner reaction, her resigned yet positive practicality, all fused into a single experience. These extracts will not seem important in any thematic reading, yet they are of the essence of *Swamp Angel* as an achieved work of art.

Poise, simplicity, profundity, exquisite control of tone, delicate human insight, and above all that compassion that becomes the redeeming feature of so many of her human and therefore imperfect characters: all these are qualities that distinguish Ethel Wilson's work and are communicated through the verbal texture of her novels. One thinks of the elaborate inlaid beauty alongside the potential force of the Swamp Angel, the satisfying but delicate fragility of Maggie's yellow Chinese bowl.

85

And reference to revolver and bowl leads me to a related point. Through these recurring images and a number of others, Ethel Wilson conveys additional, often complex meanings. We call them symbols — yet how clumsy, how unsatisfactory is that word also! Merely another way of pigeon-holing that proves limiting. Ethel Wilson warns us within the novel of the inadequacy. Nell Severance wakes after her fall, remembers the crowd and its response to the revolver, and knows that the symbolic Swamp Angel must go: "All this nowadays of symbol symbol symbol . . . destroying reality . . ." (p. 79). This is not merely Nell's own interior monologue; Ethel Wilson has spoken in her own voice about the limitations of symbolism, and we know that she shares Nell's sentiments.[13] Nell renounces the Swamp Angel for the very reason that it has become emblematic and therefore unreal, and after it has been sent away Ethel Wilson remarks: "Her endeared symbol was gone and she would not touch it any more. I have nothing now but the reality, she thought stoically and fairly cheerfully . . ." (p. 83). It is a redeeming act, and it reminds us, as serious readers, that our very terminology, in its attractiveness and convenience, can become reductively simplifying. The Swamp Angel is more than a symbol in being itself.

IV

My time is almost exhausted, but I must give a few minutes' attention to one more novel. So far, my examples have been drawn from familiar and established works. But it is a responsibility of criticism to be able to assess the contemporary, and I feel the need to comment briefly on a novel that has not yet found a recognized, undisputed place in enduring Canadian fiction. One published within the last twelve months proves admirably suited to my purpose since its qualities cannot in my opinion be properly revealed by the thematic approach. I refer to Jack Hodgins' *The Invention of the World*.

This novel portrays and explores two human communities: the Revelations Colony of Truth, a peculiar quasi-religious group founded by Donal Keneally, a "messiah-monster,"[14] on Vancouver Island at the turn of the century, and a collection of idiosyncratic misfits and their acquaintances who occupy the site of the defunct colony in the early 1970s. Superficially, this loosely knit organization appears to provide no more than a minimal framework roughly linking a collection of separable short stories. Indeed, one is tempted to suggest *Spit Delaney's Island Revisited* as a suitable title. But further consideration shows that this greatly underestimates the subtlety of Hodgins' art.

On a first reading, while brooding over the subject of this paper, I found myself doubting whether any thematic significance could be read into the novel at all. But that, I now see, would be mistaken. Keneally's bringing over the whole population of an Irish village to create a new life and a new community in Canada obviously has nationalist and historical implications, while the suggestion that they may in fact only exchange "one madman-master for another" (p. 97) forms the basis for a possible political allegory. The problem they face on arrival — "How was it possible to turn this forest into a piece of land where they could do the only thing they knew how to do, which was farm?" (p. 116) — becomes an archetypal version of the pioneer-theme, and it is by no means accidental that their successors on the property, Maggie Kyle and the "collection of losers" she gathers round her, are referred to as "the new pioneers" (p. 264). Moreover, the fact that the site of the colony becomes a modern trailer-park patronized by "American tourists who spend their time out on the strait catching salmon to take home with them" (p. xi) clearly strikes a number of sensitive contemporary chords.

This kind of approach could be extended, but ultimately such interpretations prove unsatisfying. When one of the immigrants insists that the hero of the land to which they are sailing is "a fine big red-nosed Irishman named Sir Sean A. McDermott" (p. 112), we realize that it would be easy to take this kind of meaning too solemnly. And one would have to be unusually insensitive not to respond to the bubbling exuberance that pulses through the whole novel. How can we come to terms with the elusive, pigeon-hole-defying richness of this book?

The real title — not *Spit Delaney's Island Revisited*, but *The Invention of the World* — may give us the clue we need. Who does the inventing? There are, I think, four answers (all doubtless correct): (1) Donal Keneally, who claims to keep God in his pocket and, as founder of the Colony, brings his people to "all the world that anyone ever needs" (p. 253); (2) Maggie Kyle, mother, bride, and "loggers' whore" (p. 342), who occupies the central place in the novel and who, indispensable to her collection of losers, proves a positive, humane, beneficent alternative to Keneally; (3) Strabo Becker, who "wants to be God" and, armed with notebook and tape-recorder, goes out to interview, to collect and preserve the records out of which the story is built (of him we are told: "Sometimes this god-man almost believes that he owns this island, that he has perhaps invented it . . . a shy man, who knows only this much: that the tale . . . exists somewhere at the centre of his gathered hoard, in the confusion of tales and lies and protests and legends and exaggerations" [pp. x-xi]); and (4) — of course — Jack Hodgins himself who, by creating the novel, has invented not only its world but Keneally, Maggie, and Becker as well.

But it is, of course, a world built out of words, and the world is vivid and memorable because Hodgins' words are also. Stylistically, the book is a *tour de force*. As every reader must have noted, the story of the journey from Ireland and the founding of the Colony is told as if it were a Celtic myth in that Irish vernacular lilt that comes to us through William Carleton, Charles Lever, Lady Gregory's "Kiltartanese," and all the verbal blarney of the Irish Literary Revival. And the central section, "Scrapbook," is Becker's scrapbook in which he types up the recorded statements of his interviewees (who subject the Colony to a many-angled analysis reminiscent of Browning in *The Ring and the Book*), and thus preserves the individual speech rhythms of a varied cross-section of Vancouver Island residents. Throughout, Hodgins' own ear for varieties of speech is manifest in the crisp, differentiated dialogue; and above all we enjoy his controlled, limpid, exquisitely modulated, but direct and natural-sounding prose. Like Ethel Wilson, Hodgins controls his novel both formally and stylistically: he unifies his plot by showing how Maggie Kyle and her friends can only come to terms with their own problems after coming to terms with Keneally's colony, which constitutes the past of their world; and for all the stylistic variety, we sense the continuing presence of Hodgins' verbal discipline behind the work.

Hodgins' style cannot be properly illustrated because it shifts and adapts with such astonishing ease to the requirements of his subject. Here, then, is a quotation offered not as a representative illustration, but as a (not *quite* random) sample:

They drove north, mostly north, for more than two hours. They moved slowly at first, out of town, down around the highrise apartment block and across the bridge and out past

the string of service-stations and take-out restaurants and
motels that stood where until recently there had been the high
old houses and flower gardens of the town's pioneers. . . .
Faster now, on a widened highway, they passed a long series
of sprawled-out new-car lots and the long wall of wrecked
cars piled ten high, and passed between the two sky-reflecting
lakes. Faster still, the hood flapping and shuddering, the tires
whining, they roared up through roadside stands of timber
and gouged-out subdivisions and trailer sales, out into
country, and farms, then dipped down to follow the edge of
the strait, a thumbprint bay, where the broken barnacled
posts and piles of rubble from an abandoned sawmill lay in
the beach gravel and the lace froth of the water's edge, passed
a long line of freight cars thundering south on the tracks, and
swelled up again to the top of a hill to snake through a village
where a woman in a blue-flowered dress stopped walking on
the shoulder to watch them go by. In the mirror Maggie saw
her turn, a thick woman with her hair in rollers, to waddle
stiffly away on her short white legs.

    North. She needed no maps for this journey. . . . (pp.
324-25)

    That represents Jack Hodgins' "world," microcosm and
macrocosm, regional and universal, and, although it suggests a
modern (and a quintessentially Canadian) landscape, it is nonetheless his "invention" — what he calls "an imitation world that hid a
multitude of unsuspected, unfamiliar things" (p. 107). It is made
not from themes, but from words. And this brings me (you will be
relieved to hear) to my final point. The "world" of a novel is never
identical with the "real" world that it reflects. Often, given the
Realistic convention that still (and perhaps inevitably) dominates
the novel-form, it may seem remarkably similar to the one we inhabit, but there remains always an essential difference. It is a world
of imagination, and it is therefore subject, not to the laws of this
world, but to those of art. I am not going to launch into pomposi-
ties about "the verbal universe" because such discussion soon becomes arid. I merely point out that the thematic approach to literature, whatever lip-service it may pay to Imagination, Creativity,
etc., etc., ultimately reads the world of art as if it were our own —
reduces it, I would say, to our terms. True, we should never separate the two worlds — the existence and necessity of art depends
upon the connection — but we must approach the world of art

(here, the subsidiary world of fiction) humbly and flexibly, always taking care to remain faithful to the materials from which it is created. For literature in general — and, for our purposes, the novel in particular — the materials are words (with, once again, their tones, rhythms, associations, and implications). If we neglect them — and the thematic approach does, alas, undervalue them — we are neglecting the vital ingredients of that invented world.

NOTES

1 Frank Davey, "Surviving the Paraphrase," *Canadian Literature*, No. 70 (Autumn 1976), p. 5. All further references to this work appear in the text.
2 David Arnason, ed., *Nineteenth Century Canadian Stories* (Toronto: Macmillan, 1976), p. viii.
3 Victor Hoar, *Morley Callaghan* (Toronto: Copp Clark, 1969), p. 1.
4 W. J. Keith, "The Art of Frederick Philip Grove: *Settlers of the Marsh* as an Example," *Journal of Canadian Studies*, 9, No. 2 (Aug. 1974), 26-36.
5 Frederick Philip Grove, *Our Daily Bread* (1928; rpt. New Canadian Library, No. 114, Toronto: McClelland and Stewart, 1975), p. 178.
6 John Moss, *Sex and Violence in the Canadian Novel: The Ancestral Present* (Toronto: McClelland and Stewart, 1977), p. 23.
7 Margaret Atwood, *Survival: A Thematic Guide to Canadian Literature* (Toronto: House of Anansi, 1972), p. 206.
8 D. G. Jones, *Butterfly on Rock: A Study of Themes and Images in Canadian Literature* (Toronto: Univ. of Toronto Press, 1970), p. 66.
9 Morley Callaghan, *Such Is My Beloved* (1934; rpt. New Canadian Library, No. 2, Toronto: McClelland and Stewart, 1957), p. 129. All further references to this work appear in the text.
10 A registrant at the conference suggested to me after my lecture that "the girls" might well imply "prostitutes" in Callaghan's period and place. This possibility should be considered, though a rereading of the novel with the suggestion in mind did not convince me of its likelihood. It cannot surely be intended in the passage quoted in the next paragraph of my text. And even if the possibility is allowed, the fact remains that (unlike some of his commentators) Callaghan chose the neutral word that need not carry secondary implications.
11 Ethel Wilson, *Swamp Angel* (1957; rpt. New Canadian Library, No. 29, Toronto: McClelland and Stewart, 1962), p. 128. All further references to this work appear in the text.

¹² Desmond Pacey, Introduction, in *Swamp Angel*, by Ethel Wilson, New Canadian Library, No. 29 (Toronto: McClelland and Stewart, 1962), p. 7.

¹³ See Desmond Pacey, *Ethel Wilson* (New York: Twayne, 1967), p. 36.

¹⁴ Jack Hodgins, *The Invention of the World* (Toronto: Macmillan, 1977), p. 120. All further references to this work appear in the text.

HENRY KREISEL

In the 1960s the women's movement, or the women's liberation movement as it came to be known, took centre stage. I found myself from the beginning in sympathy with the aims of that movement. I therefore read a good deal of what articulate women were writing, from the publication of Betty Friedan's *The Feminine Mystique* until later, when more radical voices began to be heard. I was particularly interested in the analyses, mostly thematic, that women critics made of literary works. The analyses by women critics such as Kate Millett of D. H. Lawrence and of Henry Miller made a profound impression on me because they read these works, which I thought I knew well, in a new way and with a new emphasis, and they took me back to the texts so that I found myself reading Lawrence again with new eyes; they had brought to the analysis of the themes of the Lawrencian opus insights which I, though I had read Lawrence for twenty years, was not aware of or had skipped. So I was brought back to the word.

I agree with Bill Keith when he said that we must ultimately look at the text; he gave an admirable example of how that kind of analysis should be conducted when he analyzed Ethel Wilson's *Swamp Angel*. Re-evaluation is an ongoing critical process. As I said, one can, through thematic analysis, find oneself returning to the text. And, if one of the functions of literature is the raising of consciousness with the creation of awareness, then one method may be as good as another. What Professor Keith has done is important as a corrective perhaps, but I would not therefore like to say, as he seems to say, or implies at any rate, that thematic studies are the least promising way of coming to terms with Canadian fiction. I am not yet convinced that that is so. It is one important way. For that reason, M. H. Abrams' definition is too limiting, because

Abrams puts the emphasis upon thesis or the didacticism of a work. Insofar as thematic criticism tends to become thesis criticism, I would fully agree with Professor Keith that we ought to blow the whistle. I agree when he says that grand generalizations are often derived from small and perhaps not particularly fruitful examples. But that is a function of the critic, not a function of the method. If a critic is judicious, if the conclusions he or she derives from his or her reading arise naturally from the material, if he or she does not impose a vision upon the material, then I think the method can be very fruitful. No method guarantees results. There is Northrop Frye, and there are the little fry; there are good critics and bad.

The same thing goes for linguistic inadequacy. I agree with Professor Keith that critics are often linguistically inadequate, both in their own expression and in the way that they read. That again is not a function of method but a function of the critic. I have read people who try to do the kind of analysis that Professor Keith has done with *Swamp Angel*, and it was disastrous, linguistically, and in every other way. I want to say something about linguistic usage while I think about it. Professor Keith was particularly effective in one way when he concentrated on Morley Callaghan's use of "the girls" — "girls" rather than "prostitutes." Let me tell you a story. I came to Canada in 1940-41 in a rather unusual way, as a civilian internee, because I had come from Austria to England and, in England, Austrian and German nationals were interned at the beginning of the war and many of them came to Canada in that way. So, for about two years, from my eighteenth to my twentieth year, I was interned in Quebec and New Brunswick, and for those two years, I saw no women, spoke to no women. When I finally arrived in Toronto in 1942, I was hungry for female companionship. I lived in a medical fraternity, and after about two weeks I said to one of the students, "I badly need a girl." He said, "What? You need a girl, go to Jarvis Street." Jarvis Street was the hangout of prostitutes. I didn't know that at the time. I went to Jarvis Street and saw the girls. But that was not what I meant at all. I just wanted to say that Callaghan wrote during that period and one would have to see how the term "the girls" was used in the prim Torontonian atmosphere of the late thirties and forties. I suspect that some of the euphemism that is embodied in that term is in his book, but I would have to look at the text carefully. Linguistic approaches are very important, but one has to be careful. It is more than a matter of words on a page. We hear voices rising from the page and they do tell us something. And the world that they paint is related to the world that we know, but not precisely the world that we know.

One other point. There's an implication in Professor Keith's paper, because he quotes Frank Davey with approval, that other countries do not generalize, do not use the thematic approach. Other countries do, very extensively. I am quite familiar with German criticism of the nineteenth and twentieth centuries, and the Germans loved to theorize; German critics created so many pigeon-holes, the birds didn't have any room to fly. And Bob Kroetsch referred yesterday to the impact of D. H. Lawrence's *Studies in Classic American Literature*. Lawrence was not an academic critic, but his work was essential, because what he did was to brush away a lot of the inessentials, to try to see what the shape and pattern of American literature was. One does not necessarily agree with him, but that does not matter. Such attempts are essential for a national literature. It is essential for the creation of a consciousness to know what the overall shape, the overall pattern of the literature, of the life, is. To that extent I see literature and life interpenetrating very closely and, therefore, I would not like to do away with that approach. All the same, it is now very important that the mature works of our literature, many of which have been created in the extraordinary renaissance of the last fifteen to twenty years, be examined carefully in structural and linguistic terms. I agree with Doug Jones that we do not all have to do this with everything, but some of our critics ought to do it so that the rest of us can benefit.

D. G. JONES

The first problem we have is to reply to the assumptions and observations of Bill Keith. Basically, one has no quarrel with anyone who has the time, interest, and energy to attend carefully and minutely to a book. Even a critic would like to have his book read with that ideal attention. And, if we're ever going to find out anything about the precise nature and value of an individual book, story, poem, this is the way it will have to be read. This does not deny the validity of looking at larger patterns, whether of themes or of forms.

It is significant to recognize large patterns. It is interesting to talk about what happened generally in the Romantic period, or to say that there is something generally characteristic of Baroque literature. Also interesting was a recent observation that Thomas Pynchon's *The Crying of Lot 49* and *Gravity's Rainbow* use a fictional device called "God games," which links Thomas Pynchon with Hermann Hesse, with Miguel de Cervantes, with Lope de Vega. This linking of various novels over several hundred years is significant.

When I wrote a book which has been called a piece of thematic criticism I was certainly concerned with large patterns. At the time there did not seem to be any books of that sort; perhaps now there are too many. But this does not prevent other people from writing other kinds of books. I shall continue to look at large patterns because I compare English- and French-Canadian literatures, and if you are going to compare two literatures which have not talked to each other for most of their existence, what can you compare? Not mutual influences. And it is difficult to compare individual writers in some of the traditional ways. But certain larger patterns do characterize the two literatures.

I could demonstrate at this point in time the consistency of English- and French-Canadian poetry over the last 150 years, that both have remained faithful to a certain basic vision within their distinct collective cultural imaginations. I could illustrate this consistency both in terms of theme and in terms of form. English-Canadian poetry, as Dorothy Livesay has observed, has emphasized the documentary, or narrative, poem from the nineteenth century to the present. This form tends to reflect a horizontal vision, a vision of a world busy extending its civilization in one direction or another. The hero of that poem was originally the axeman: he is the man who builds a civilization in a horizontal world. As the poetry develops, conflicts and ambiguities in that vision develop, as well as contradictions. The great ambiguity evident from the very beginning in nineteenth-century poems is the ambiguity of a man who comes along to build a rising village, a great city, several great cities, and simultaneously attempts to preserve rural virtues. One can look at the figures in English-Canadian poetry and note that they are metonymical (after Roman Jakobsen's distinction between metaphor and metonymy). In a sense, that means that the English-Canadian poet is rather prosaic: he makes surveys, is always talking about particular places and particular things, has catalogues.

94

In French-Canadian poetry you find a totally different kind of hero. As Naïm Kattan said yesterday, he's a man who looks nostalgically at the past. He is witness to a lost ideal, which tends ever to be elsewhere, particularly in a metaphysical beyond. The poles of the French-Canadian poet's world are vertical rather than horizontal; they move from heaven to earth rather than across the earth. His ideal would be to inhabit a spiritual reality, which he can never manage to do. Consequently, his form of expression differs from that of the English-Canadian poet; it is much more metaphorical. If you read an Alain Grandbois poem, even though its author may happen to be travelling all over the world, you never know where precisely Grandbois or the voice in the poem happens to be. Even when the French-Canadian poets during the '60s began to celebrate the land, one kept looking for poems about precise places, precise individuals, as in English-Canadian poems, and they did not appear. There are no lists, no catalogues of a type similar to those in English-Canadian poetry.

It is therefore evident from the poetry that there are distinctive cultural imaginations which have dominated both bodies of poetry for more than one hundred years. I haven't explored this in the novel, but I would expect these patterns to be similarly reflected in that genre as well. One can go from poetry to the novel, however, by noting the following pattern. For several generations French-Canadian poetry was haunted by the ghosts of the past, whereas English-Canadian poetry boasted relatively few. During the last generation this picture has been reversed. French-Canadian poets now emphasize the future; English-Canadian poets — Al Purdy, Margaret Atwood, Dennis Lee — have increasingly focussed on the past; they have begun to recover the ghostly farms, villages, voices of earlier inhabitants. In Lee's "Civil Elegies" the ancestral shades swarm like the eumenides, furies, into the square in front of Toronto's City Hall. These ghosts, shades, eumenides, furies, that were our ancestors, float, fill the air, and cry out as in the French-Canadian poetry. But in French Canada poets are now emphasizing the future.

Exactly the same thing is happening in the Canadian novel. A concern to rediscover the past is clearly represented in Margaret Laurence's *The Diviners*, Rudy Wiebe's *The Temptations of Big Bear*, even in Margaret Atwood's *Surfacing*, although there the concern is more theoretical, more allegorical. The pattern is observable, demonstrable, and to recognize its presence and trace its outlines is illuminating for the literature and for ourselves.

The recognition of general patterns is, as Barry Cameron suggested yesterday, the critical observation of significance. It demonstrates the relationship of books to each other, and of books to culture and society, and it tells us something about the general character of our imaginative life and of our society. That is a very worthwhile achievement. The process might, I agree, include books that are bad as well as books that are excellent, but that does not in any way lessen the importance and significance of the pattern. It is, of course, also important to discriminate good from bad books, but that is a different exercise. One can only do one thing at a time.

LAURIE RICOU

Although we are intended, I assume, to lock horns in battle like moose in mating season, my quarrel is not to any great extent with what Bill Keith has said. He has been, as a good Canadian critic must be, careful, judicious, and sensible. Furthermore, he is one of my former professors, which has two implications: one is that he still intimidates me, and the other is that it is from him that I began to learn, however inadequately, the craft of criticism. Furthermore, I was educated in part at the University of Toronto, which brings with it the automatic and rather horrifying label of Frygian, a term I've never quite understood. It may have, come to think of it, something to do with moose knee-deep in northern swamps. No, my quarrel is not with Professor Keith specifically, although there are certain implications in his paper with which my presentation will appear to quarrel. It is really with a current attitude in Canadian criticism; in fact, it seems to me that the attitude which Professor Keith articulates in his paper has gained a good deal more currency in the field of Canadian criticism than he would suggest. My quarrel is with the Procrustean bed school of critics on Canadian criticism. They are revealed in the rush to these microphones to denounce thematic criticism (to deny that we were or had been thematic critics).

I use Procrustean bed because that is the favorite metaphor of this school. Its argument goes like this: it insists on stretching the limbs of Canadian critics in order to assign them forever to the bed of thematic criticism. The thing itself, thematic criticism, may not even exist, as Professor Keith implied, but the term is being used to turn criticism on Canadian criticism into a "huge debunking project."[1] This Procrustean bed school is likely to ignore, for example, that its *bête noire*, Northrop Frye, is the very man who insists in the *Anatomy of Criticism: Four Essays* that in literature questions of fact or truth are subordinated to the primary literary aim of producing a structure of words for its own sake. Frye is dismissed, or almost dismissed, because of his "thematic bias"[2] and the fact that he was treating Canadian writing as "serious litera ture," discussing the particularities of its language, the nuances of its metaphors, metrics, and rhythms, before most of us were old enough, or bothered, to ask whether there was a Canadian literature at all is completely ignored.

Doug Jones is similarly stretched on the Procrustean bed when *Butterfly on Rock: A Study of Themes and Images in Canadian Literature* is categorized as "documenting localized . . . concerns" and "violat[ing] the harmony of form and content."[3] This sort of pigeon-holing ignores the pervasive, if indirect, way in which a poet's interpretations illuminate the subtleties of each writer's language. The poet's sensibility is everywhere in *Butterfly on Rock* and we should not ignore it. Jones has much to say about language and craft. The book gives insight, for example, into Birney's use of tone in "El Greco: Espolio," into Grove's use of the term "civilization," into point of view in McDougall's *Execution*, and one could go on.[4]

Sometimes I fear that the Procrustean bed school of criticism might dismiss M. H. Abrams' *The Mirror and the Lamp* because it sees a pattern in autonomous works of literature, or Edward Partridge's *The Broken Compass: A Study of the Major Comedies of Ben Jonson*, which is a study of metaphor, because its title must mean that the book is obsessed with lack of direction. Criticism, after all, should make the reading of a work of literature a fuller, richer experience. We should evaluate a work of criticism, then, by its ability to enable reading. Analytical, stylistic criticism may be just as sterile, as unilluminating, as what we have been calling thematic criticism. If you look at some of the articles in *Critical Inquiry*, you'll see that quickly enough. Just as the writer who limits himself to solving technical problems will lapse into inappropriate effect, so the critic who looks through the microscope at language will frequently torture words and distort the total effect of the work at which he is looking. There are obvious limitations, as Margaret Atwood reminds us in *The Edible Woman*, both to a monograph on womb symbols in Beatrix Potter *and* a term paper on monosyllables in Milton. On the other hand, we must admit that thematic criticism, or at least the range of approaches that we are reducing here under that term, is essential. Professor Keith tells us that by devoting six pages to a discussion of the meaning of *The Swamp Angel* as preparation for two and one half pages on stylistic effect.

As for a particular novel, so for an entire literature. The discussion of theme and meaning must precede more careful comment on verbal nuance. Language, unlike paint, is used by almost everybody in almost every kind of situation. Furthermore, the novel, of all literary genres, is the social genre; it has its origins in popular social contexts. It is a literary structure which gives us, more nearly than any other, the whole sense of an experience. It is, or was, the most popular of genres. The critic who turns the novel into an exercise in verbal ingenuity will miss literature's impurity, will miss, that is, the very source of its strength. My simple conclusion is that we are in some danger in this country, as our attempt to find the ten best Canadian novels might also suggest, in assuming that there is one right way for criticism, of declaring an orthodoxy from which no variation is allowed. But what our literature, all literature, demands is criticism which finds its validity in making reading a fuller, more profound, more meaningful, more magical experience. Rather than being prescriptive about our criticism, we should encourage Marxist criticism, cultural criticism, Post-Modernist criticism, historical criticism, aesthetic criticism, Structuralist criticism, and you can extend the list on and on. In short, we need a diversity of critical approaches which will celebrate and make available the richness of our literature and the variety of contexts from which it has emerged.

NOTES

1 Northrop Frye, "Conclusion," in *Literary History of Canada: Canadian Literature in English*, gen. ed. and introd. Carl F. Klinck (Toronto: Univ. of Toronto Press, 1965), p. 821. Frye speaks, of course, of a possibility for Canadian literary criticism *per se*.
2 Frank Davey, *From There to Here: A Guide to English Canadian Literature since 1960*, Vol. II of *Our Nature — Our Voices* (Erin, Ont.:

Porcépic, 1974), p. 22.

[3] Barry Cameron and Michael Dixon, "Introduction," *Minus Canadian: Penultimate Essays in Literature, Studies in Canadian Literature*, 2 (Summer 1977), 140.

[4] D. G. Jones, *Butterfly on Rock: A Study of Themes and Images in Canadian Literature* (Toronto: Univ. of Toronto Press, 1970), pp. 73, 126, 141-42.

JOHN MOSS

I don't think we should take ourselves here or in the audience too solemnly at this conference or at any conference. The important thing is the novel, not the novelist, and certainly not the critic. Let's not be too solemn about this and let's name names. I'm not sure why we must be careful, judicious, sensible. We can't "not name" the authors of books.

Professor Keith's paper I enjoyed very much. It was very intelligent, very sensitive, particularly in its actual readings of novels. I share with him the problem of not knowing what themes are and thematic criticism is. Here today we've heard theme to mean story, subject-matter, thesis, motif, meaning, something to do with interdisciplinary aesthetics, and something to do with pigeons. I don't think of myself as a thematic critic but I might be. It seems to me that a thematic critic is really a critic who criticizes critics on a thematic basis. I'm fascinated by the response of people who lump very different critics together as thematic critics. Professor Keith does this to some extent, and certainly Frank Davey does it in his article in *Canadian Literature*. Their approach to the critics is a thematic approach. They assume that the so-called thematic critic can only be concerned with theme, not with shape, form, language. I feel very unread at this point. Surely I recognize in my criticism that apples are red, but also that they are soft or hard, tasty, expensive, and possibly symbolic. The failure to recognize that I do so constitutes textual irresponsibility.

These critics also assume that theme is somehow thought by the so-called thematic critics to be an aesthetic criterion, a criterion of excellence. If that were true, *Sex and Violence in the Canadian Novel* should have established as the great Canadian novel the one with the most orgasms, or the one with the most mutilations. They

99

further assume that the so-called thematic critic is claming exclusivity: isolation, or survival, as uniquely Canadian. No responsible critic claims such exclusivity; we are aware of universality, but I am also concerned with its particular patterns in our literature. George Woodcock's review of *Patterns of Isolation*, I remember, failed to recognize this awareness. Textual irresponsibility disturbs me, particularly that of the Davey article, which wrenches phrases from context, distorts emphasis, distorts balance, all for the sake of generalization. Professor Keith uses the term "habitual procedures"; if he used that term about Ethel Wilson or Jack Hodgins, you would dismiss him. Professor Keith says that the so-called thematic critics ignore emphasis on word and language, and do not evaluate. That is simply wrong. I, for one, do evaluate, both implicitly and explicitly, in *Patterns of Isolation* and *Sex and Violence in the Canadian Novel*. As for the lack of emphasis on words, that criticism is irresponsible unless supported by specific reference to text. The same cavalier attitude leads Davey to say that my criticism is largely derivative of Frye and Jones. I am not a small Frye. I am quite capable of being good or bad on my own. (This same Davey includes Gwethalyn Graham in his book *From There to Here: A Guide to English Canadian Literature since 1960* solely on thematic grounds!)

Professor Keith says that you cannot be thematic in approaching Hodgins' *The Invention of the World*, and then shows how the book holds together in terms of the theme of creation. His reading of *Swamp Angel* was very sensitive, very intelligent, but was surely thematic. Likewise his representation of *Our Daily Bread*. The study of themes can be useful; themes can get us involved with literature; they can provide a context for reading, or a perspective from which to read; they can open up the past to the present. Surely this is worthwhile both to reader and writer. But criticism based unduly on themes can produce problems. As Ronald Sutherland has it, Quebec is reduced to a region. As Warren Tallman has it, disguising his criticism in poetic rhetoric, Canada is reduced to a direction. I'm damned if I'm only a direction. Or defined by regionality.

I deny the concept imposed upon me of thematic critic, but I do not deny theme; or word, or space, or language, or passion, or reason, or vision. I demand responsible reading of my criticism and I demand that criticism of it be specific. Critics of criticism should not be less responsible than the critics they criticize.

DISCUSSION

The third session's discussion was lively. It began with rebuttal of the panelists, especially of John Moss by W. J. Keith, who suggested that anyone entitling his book *Sex and Violence in the Canadian Novel* invites the designation of thematic critic. Keith went on to say that he was emphasizing in his paper not the theme *per se* but the manner of its presentation. He concluded his rebuttal by proclaiming himself a "critical relativist," and by again insisting that "it doesn't matter what kind of criticism you ultimately do, but you must maintain a relationship to the text." Later in the discussion he qualified this suggestion of critical latitude by announcing that "we've got to the stage where we have so many first-rate novels, that the critic hasn't time to consider anything else." Moss agreed that anyone pretending to the title of literary critic, as opposed to that of cultural historian or some other cognomen, must maintain his focus, first and foremost, on the text itself. D. G. Jones, meanwhile, continued to argue for the validity of the critic's consideration of fiction of inferior quality, asserting that such work may very well contribute significantly to the description of the "imaginative house" in which we live.

The discussion then moved quickly in the direction of feminist criticism or, simply, literary criticism by women. Various members of the panel were chastised for expressing unconscious sexism and conference organizers were chastised for the modest presence of women on the panels. There was a brief consideration as to whether or not feminist criticism was thematic criticism, and Ricou pointed out that the attacks on thematic criticism, if successful, would very likely take down with them such new forms of criticism as feminist criticism.

The third session concluded with author James Houston's benediction for critics in which he announced that he found critics valuable sources of evaluation.

SESSION FOUR: Friday Afternoon, February 17, 1978

Eli Mandel: The Regional Novel: Borderline Art
Panel
Marian Engel
Frank Watt
Rudy Wiebe
Robert McDougall
Discussion

The Regional Novel: Borderline Art

ELI MANDEL

Some time after I began this paper I came across a remark of John Berryman's which, I thought, should serve as my epigraph. "In some very serious sense," he says, "there is no competition either on Parnassus or on the hard way up there." A line from one of Michael Ondaatje's poems stays with me too. It is from his poem "White Dwarfs," perhaps a meditation on getting out, breaking loose, perhaps going mad — anyhow, like Buddy Bolden the hero of Ondaatje's *Coming Through Slaughter*, walking right out of the picture almost as casually as one walked into it, though certainly with pain. "Why do I love most / among my heroes," Ondaatje writes, "those / who sail to that perfect edge / where there is no social fuel." The line is echoed in *Coming Through Slaughter*, "they had talked for hours moving gradually off the edge of the social world."

When I began to think of what I would say to you about "the regional novel" today, I thought first this would be another version of "social fuel": Canadian regionalism, geographical divisions, cultural divides, centralist and hinterland tensions; the subject invites such mapping. It looks, after all, as if it should be about the writer and place, the writer and history, the writer in his place, hardly anything like the romantic alienation of the heroes loved by Ondaatje, or the intensity achieved in such high, lonely places as the ones they sail to. But initial certainties begin to blur. Perhaps because certainties about place begin to blur. Sometimes regionalism is linked to provincialism, especially in a country like ours with its provinces that do claim allegiance. There is the example of Quebec, after all. My own experience, perhaps atypical, is instructive — to me at least. Among the first anthologies to include one of my poems was Carlyle King's *Saskatchewan Harvest: A Golden Jubilee Selection of Song and Story*; later I was allowed, as a peripheral case, into Laurie Ricou's *Twelve Prairie Poets: 87 Prairie Poems*, but the more recent *Number One Northern: Poetry from Saskatchewan*, with some forty poets from Saskatchewan, remains suspicious of my apostasy in Toronto and excludes me. Once, an odd-sounding collection entitled *English Poets from Quebec* included my work though by then I had lived in Edmonton for six years and was teaching at Glendon College in Toronto. By 1967 my suspect record must have begun to make itself known. Having returned to Alberta once again and left still another time, I was refused admission to a proposed Alberta centenary anthology until I had taken a kind of loyalty oath, swearing out an affidavit that I was in deed and in truth an Alberta poet. Maybe it's not odd, then, that my present version of regional writing vacillates between the idiosyncratic and the representative, between the general, social context and whatever is out toward, or back in to more and more particular, I would even say quirky versions of experience. Or perhaps more precisely, I would want to begin with what I'll call the evaluative, political, and theoretical questions that this subject and this conference raise before I venture any comments on regional novels.

Questions of evaluation get themselves confused with the politics and theory of regionalism. But since presumably we address ourselves here to achievements in fiction, it's probably just as well to begin with an instructive reminder that the regional novel and regional writing, whatever peculiar status might attach to that qualifier today (and of that one cannot be certain), have not always stood in high repute among Canadian critics. No need to rehearse the history of the term. Two influential writers serve to make the point. In his justly influential review of A. J. M. Smith's *Book of Canadian Poetry: A Critical and Historical Anthology*, Northrop Frye connects regionalism with colonialism, the imperial side of that equation splitting the English away from the French who, Frye comments, specialize in "the regional aspects." "The province or region," he says ". . . is usually a vestigial curiosity to be written up by some nostalgic tourist." E. K. Brown's equally important comments on Canadian poetry dwell on forces telling against the growth of a national literature, including a strongly particularist and regionalist art he sees as a possible stage in Canadian writing following World War II. And though he welcomes the cultural maturity that should develop from "a set of novels, sketches or memoirs that [would describe] the life of Canadian towns and cities as it really is," he believes "In the end . . . regionalist art will fail because it stresses the superficial and peculiar at the expense, at least, if not to the exclusion, of the fundamental and universal."

It matters little, I think, that Frye's reservations then were based on a relatively simplistic reading of Canadian history, which he has since greatly modified, or that Brown's developed from a prescient view of the direction of contemporary political and social developments. For both, "regional" implied the same literary objection: superficiality. The question remains today of rethinking the values of regional writing in the light, one would hope, of contemporary achievement. At the least, an attempt at evaluation implies some sort of continuing tension between the national and the regional in literature as in politics.

The subject poses political questions. I wonder whether the conference in its concern for the evaluation of fiction in what is purported to be a national context has raised the problem of literature in languages other than English. One of the political manoeuvres, which we'll have reason to consider in a moment, used to deflate political tensions implicit in any claims made for the value of regionalism is to detach cultural considerations from political ones, to distinguish, as Professor Frye does, between imaginative identity and political unity, or to describe the essential meaning of Canada as the balance between the two. But important as the argument is, one wonders whether it really skirts the oddity that arguments for cultural nationalism and cultural separatism tend to be identical in form, differing in content. It is, I submit, the dilemma of this paper that to argue for the value of regionalism is, in part, to subvert the apparent aim of the conference.

The political question has other dimensions somewhat to the side of my direct concerns, but I raise them since they bear on the question of evaluation, listing by merit, balloting, or what have

105

you. The point I want to make here has to do with the difference between critical demands, properly speaking, and pragmatic demands. They will be familiar to you, phrased more gracefully and more precisely in Matthew Arnold's distinction between *culture* and *power*, a distinction to which I'll return in the course of this paper.

Arnold cites "a very clever writer," a Mr. Harrison, who develops a thesis about culture,

> Perhaps the very silliest cant of the day, said Mr. Frederic Harrison, is the cant about culture. Culture is a desirable quality in a critic of new books, and sits well on a possessor of *belles lettres*; but as applied to politics, it means simply a turn for small fault-finding, love of selfish ease, and indecision in actions. The man of culture is in politics one of the poorest mortals alive. For simple pedantry and want of good sense no man is his equal. No assumption is too unreal, no end is too unpractical for him. But the active exercise of politics requires common sense, sympathy, trust, resolution, and enthusiasm, qualities which your man of culture has carefully rooted out, lest they damage the delicacy of his critical olfactories. Perhaps they are the only class of responsible beings in the community who cannot with safety be entrusted with power.

Arnold's comment on Harrison's remarks might remind us of our own responsibilities: "Now for my part I do not wish to see men of culture asking to be entrusted with power; and, indeed, I have freely said, that in my opinion the speech most proper, at present, for a man of culture to make to a body of his fellow-countrymen who get him into a committee-room is Socrates's: *Know Thyself.*"

Let me put the point this way, as it bears on our deliberations here. Is there not a distinction to be made between criticism, properly speaking, and the demands of the curriculum? Is there not a distinction to be made between criticism, properly speaking, and the demands of the publisher? Is there not a distinction to be made between criticism, properly speaking, and the demands for an establishment or an orthodoxy? It would seem to me that disinterestedness and detachment require at the very least some remoteness from the demands of curriculum, publishing, and orthodoxy. And it would seem to me that the political implications of establishing lists sit oddly not only or simply with regional identification but as well and particularly with the kinds of openness ordinarily associated with criticism and creativity. This is not said, I trust, out of the narrow bias which might attend my arguing a point about regional interests but from the broader base of critical theory itself.

Theoretical questions do not arise simply for the sake of identification. An amorphous uncertain notion at best — are we talking of a genre? A mode? A style? — regionalism is not likely to offer opportunities for clarity. Questions arise simply out of the need to disentangle a knot of possibilities. Are we concerned, for example, with local colour, historical romance, the farm story, the idyll, mythic form, the literature of the small town, the created "world" of the writer? This may seem an inverted way of approaching the subject but I suggest the need to do so is imposed by the terminology itself. In short, the questions are not unlike those imposed by speaking of writing in national terms. You will recall that the Argentinian, Jorge Luis Borges, writing on "The Argentine Writer and Tradition" begins by describing the topic sceptically as "a mere rhetorical topic which lends itself to pathetic elaborations rather than . . . a true mental difficulty . . . [It is] an appearance, a simulacrum, a pseudo problem"; he resolves it accordingly: "Anything we Argentinian writers can do successfully will become part of our Argentinian tradition." Nothing is *a priori* here. This begins to suggest a particular line of inquiry and evaluation: the problem is in its statement as a problem. So long as the question of distinctiveness in regional writing is not seriously raised, one can be certain that the art itself is thought to be minor, trivial, superficial. And it is so dismissed, a superficial art. But the moment it is felt to be central, not peripheral, one can be certain the writing itself has assumed a particular character, perhaps out of its perceptions or a significant alteration in approach, or because its *historical* and *political* role has been discussed. "Why do you call Quebec writing regional?" Solange Chaput-Rolland of the Task Force on National Unity asked me of a brief I presented on "Literature and National Unity," "It is separatist, is it not?" The critical, that is theoretical question, follows on the fact of regionalism. It does not precede it.

No one, I think, can read whatever regional criticism one finds in Canada without becoming aware of a limitation at once justifiable and puzzling. It is what Laurie Ricou at the outset of his study of Canadian prairie fiction, *Vertical Man/Horizontal World: Man and Landscape in Canadian Prairie Fiction*, calls "the regional form of a question legitimately asked of all Canadian literature," the relation between writing and landscape, specifically, for his purposes, between the prairie and prairie writing. Justifiable or legitimate, I suppose, for the simple reason that the land, as literary theme and image, has increasingly occupied critical attention, prairie fiction itself, as Ricou says, illustrating "both the prevalence of the myth of the land in Canadian writing and the regional qualities which derive from the encounter with a specific distinctive landscape." Puzzling, because an otherwise increasingly sophisticated criticism settles on a primitive identification which offers as an account of a literature little but a variation on a somewhat simpleminded, not to say on occasion, an odious theme.

If we turn to Frye as a guide to this subject, and that seems reasonable enough since he is after all our foremost critic, we find that in his essays on the Canadian imagination in *The Bush Garden: Essays on the Canadian Imagination*, he talks of regionalism in geographic terms, in terms of place, with significant political overtones. Imagination is regional, vegetable, as he puts it. "There's always something vegetable about the imagination, something sharply limited in range." Imagination and place. He provides a familiar paradigm, worth quoting here:

An environment turned outward to the sea, like so much of Newfoundland, and one turned toward the inland seas, like so much of the Maritimes, are an imaginative contrast: anyone who has been conditioned by one in his earliest years can hardly become conditioned by the other in the same way. Anyone brought up on the urban plains of Southern Ontario or the gentle *pays* farmland along the south shore of the St. Lawrence may become fascinated by the great sprawling wilderness of Northern Ontario or Ungava, may move there and live with its people and become accepted as one of them, but if he paints or writes about it he will paint or write as an imaginative foreigner. And what can there be in common between an imagination nurtured on the prairies, where it is a centre of consciousness diffusing itself over a vast flat expanse stretching to the remote horizon, and one nurtured in British Columbia, where it is in the midst of gigantic trees and mountains leaping into the sky all around it and obliterating the horizon everywhere?

108

The political tactics employed here should be familiar to anyone aware of a federalist problem: how to accommodate incompatible demands within the same structure? As Frye put it: "Once . . . the two elements (the political sense of unity and the imaginative sense of locality) are confused or assimilated to each other, we get the two endemic diseases of Canadian life. Assimilating identity to unity produces the empty gestures of cultural nationalism; assimilating unity to identity produces the kind of provincial isolation which is now called separatism." Alternately, distinguishing between unity and identity allows for cultural autonomy and political unity. But the distinction becomes possible by means of a very curious theory of regionalism indeed.

One would have thought, for example, that Professor Frye's brilliantly articulated theory of imagination in *Fearful Symmetry: A Study of William Blake* and *Anatomy of Criticism: Four Essays* implies something different from a vegetable imagination or the kind of connection between the imagination and place he postulates in *The Bush Garden*. Neither vegetable, nor animal, nor mineral, imagination elsewhere in Frye is specifically human. Further, insofar as regions are to be defined, outside literature itself, certainly there is reason to think not only of political and geographic definitions but especially in Canada of historic ones. Even the prairie, one recalls, is more than physical nature, a human creation in which boundaries are redrawn with virtually the frequency in which population changes, the derrick replacing the elevator, the superhighway the cart or wagon trail, the jet trail so altering the cloudscape one notices with a start the clouds of the filmed *Who Has Seen The Wind* are those never seen in Brian O'Connal's time. As to the question of the *language* of regionalism, it simply does not enter into Frye's discussion, though presumably if one were to follow an argument like Dennis Lee's in "Cadence, Country, Silence," the distinction between nationalism and separatism loses some of its force.

My own preference for other approaches to the regional than anything like local colour should be evident now, though in several attempts I expect I have brought only confusion to the subject. The merely mythical ends, I believe, as a distinction without a difference. Borges' comments, which I noted before, in their vigorous rejection of pathetic elaboration offer a possibility that once seemed attractive to me. The Irish, like the Jewish, writer, he notes, stands in an oblique relation to the culture, Western culture, of which he or she is a part; accordingly, it is sufficient to *feel different* in order to be innovators in English culture. This is not, of course, to argue from pseudo-notions of racial pre-eminence. It is linked to the notion that the regional connects with feelings of distinctiveness presumably having historical, economic, political, cultural, *and* geographic sources. In literature, it may very well connect with growing consciousness of evolving form, the *development* of distinctiveness. The question of how one brings precision to feelings and awareness of this sort I come to in a moment. First, I pause to note two versions of the regional which, turning to questions of style and cultural history, move past the limitations of geographical definition: one, the comments of Robert Kroetsch in various interviews, reviews, and articles; the other, Wallace Stegner's in his brilliant and moving *Wolf Willow*, perhaps the one fully achieved regional work, one hesitates to call it a novel, we possess.

Kroetsch speaks of regional writing not as a matter of place so much as a matter of what he calls "voice." This moves us from mere landscape art to something else in writing, something closer to the shared assumptions of a region, something carried in the folk culture, or the unofficial culture rather than in literary traditions as such. This is in part reaction to various forms of realism; in part, a formalist theory of regionalism; in part, a theory of style. Stylistically, it calls for a renewal or revitalization of language through a turn toward spoken rather than written or literary modes. Formally, it calls for a rejection of realism and a reworking of form, presumably mythic forms since these are close to the stories of folk culture: the old story retold, "The Odyssey on dry land so to speak," as Kroetsch puts it.

These are fascinating conjectures but since Kroetsch refrains from systematic or elaborated criticism they remain tantalizing hints rather than coherently worked out theory. Moreover, since Kroetsch prefers to present himself, rather as he presents his heroes and their doubles, in ambiguous situations, the interview, for example, much of what he says is tinged with sly irony. One remembers John Berryman's comment, "a certain sly desire to baffle the onrushing critic is nearly standard in poetic temperament." Still, it was Kroetsch who reassured me that the formal problems of writing themselves do connect in peculiar ways with cultural questions: why an immigrant's rejection of history might have some bearing on western alienation, for example, or why the form of a modern poem might block the possibility of writing poetry of the prairies. But it was not until I read Stegner's *Wolf Willow* that I began to understand the full implication of language for the regional writer.

Stegner's *Wolf Willow* is many things, a history, a memoir, legend, a story and memory of the last plains frontier, as he puts it, an extraordinary account of a man and writer recalling how it was to grow up, to be a boy in a small town on the prairies. It is something else as well, and here I turn to Ann Mandel's words partly because her remarks on Stegner inform much of what I say in this paper; she says his is an account of "the function of culture in a society . . . and his own role as a writer, a book in search of himself and his own identity." It is a book of definitions, frontiers, or boundaries: the line between America and Canada; the line between plains and hills, the line between the prehistoric past, preserved in the Cypress hills, and the present; the line of water flowing north and water flowing south; between the culture of farmer and rancher; between town and plain. Boundaries. For my purposes, another set drawn is in a striking passage (I've quoted it before, in an article on regional definitions, called "Writing West," but I cite it again here because it remains the core of my argument):

> . . . every frontier child knows exactly who he is, and who his mother is, and he loves his alarm clock quite as much as if it had feathers. But then comes something else, a waddling thing with webbed feet, insisting that *it* is his mother, that he is not who he thought he was, but infinitely more, heir to swans and phoenixes. In such a town as Whitemud school superimposes five thousand years of Mediterranean culture and two thousand years of Europe upon the adapted or rediscovered simplicities of a new continent . . . If there is truth in Lawrence's assertion that America's unconscious wish has always been to destroy Europe, it is also true that from Washington Irving to William Styron, American writers have been tempted to apostasy and expatriation, toward return and fusion with the parent. It is a painful and sometimes fatal division, and the farther you are from Europe — that is, the farther you are out in the hinterlands of America — the more difficult it is. Contradictory voices tell you who you are. You grow up speaking one dialect and reading and writing another. During twenty-odd years of education and another thirty of literary practice you may learn to be nimble in the

111

King's English; yet in moments of relaxation, crisis, or surprise you fall back into the corrupted lingo that is your native tongue. Nevertheless all forces of culture and snobbery are against your *writing* by ear and making contact with your natural audience. Your natural audience, for one thing, doesn't read — it *isn't* an audience. You grow out of touch with your dialect because learning and literature lead you one way unless you consciously resist. It is only the occasional Mark Twain or Robert Frost who manages to get the authentic American tone of voice into his work. For most of us, the language of literature is to some extent unreal, because school has always been separate from life.

It has been said before, of course, and in Canadian terms. The gap between culture and nature, the European-American tension, these have been talked about from different, even opposite points of view by writers like E. K. Brown, Northrop Frye, Warren Tallman, and a host of others. It appears as the crude-fine paradox in Tallman's writing, as the tension between tarzanism and tradition in Frye's critical comments on the difference between the aboriginal and the original, as the distinction between British Colonials and the "Brooklyn-Bum Self inside every Canadian and struggling to get out," in John Sutherland's introduction to *The Other Canadians: Profiles of Six Minorities*. For my purpose, Stegner's version (just a reworking of the literature vs. life dichotomy, you might say), like Robert Kroetsch's version as I now understand it, is the important one because it focuses on a regional distinction. "The writer's subject *is* his own dilemma," I said in "Writing West." That translates into the following generality: the problem of regionalism is in its statement as a problem. Or rather, less enigmatically: a region is defined by its boundaries, regionalism consisting in the mapping of boundaries — the line between here and there, its distinctiveness. It is a peculiar art to be able to discern boundaries, borderlines, and to map them in words and images requires great literary tact. Perhaps, one speculates, this is the source of Kroetsch's unease with forms, his concern with formal problems. In any event, the simpler point is that regional boundaries are not only geographical but cultural and more. Just as the regions of Canada are in part historical creations of the nation and its existence, so their articulation is more than a historical matter, a definition of our mode of existence in Canada. Consider, for example, that the Canadian West is not only a particular geographic division but to a very large extent the creation of the so-called national policy of the federal government, which laid down not only railway tracks but also the survey and the lines of social development in its choice of an immigrant population to be committed to supplying eastern manufacturing with a market and the country with another staple for export; and, as Rudy Wiebe has so movingly and — it is not too much of a word — grandly shown us, its creation brought it into sharp conflict with those people whose vision of the nature of the West as land and home differed so greatly from those involved in its new shape that one would have thought the two were speaking of and seeing worlds apart. In 1968, in a superb account of Prairie literature, to which I'll have reason to refer once more, Henry Kreisel notes that the conquest of territory, by definition a violent process, is significantly absent from the literature he is discussing and wonders whether a conscious or subconscious process of suppression is at work. One wonders now what redefinitions of land and territory allow the repressed material to break forth so prophetically in Wiebe's work.

Obviously, the implied regional definitions mean that I would call on Canadian novels or fiction or "works" (I use the least definite term simply to preserve ambiguities) which tend to be representative, that is, self-referring or self-defining, *about* themselves so to speak, and with a great deal of regret simply would not include idylls, family chronicles, novels of local colour, allowing others to argue for them or make the case for their genuine indispensability. Think of the impoverishment, I will be told, for presumably on somewhat arbitrary pedantic grounds I would not include in the discussion the much-loved *Anne of Green Gables* or any of the Anne series, the most widely read of regional idylls; *Jalna* too would go by the wayside; a further step and Buckler's *The Mountain and the Valley* gets pitched aside; and emboldened now by this sheer recklessness, out with *Who Has Seen the Wind*, and let's not even consider the possibility of Robertson Davies, Alice Munro, Raymond Knister, Martha Ostenso, Charles Bruce, or Matt Cohen. The novel of French Canada or Quebec, of course, has not entered into consideration, partly because of language questions, partly because of political questions.

It has always been, of course, a sound rule, George Orwell's I think, to break any or all rules rather than do anything outright barbarous. In part, I mean to point to the barbarousness of an attempt at classification, in part to indicate the degree of uncertainty and confusion we enter if, so to speak, anything goes. Nothing is to be gained from trying to work out the sense of a question about whether or not *Who Has Seen the Wind* is a regional novel or whether it transcends the limitations implied or whether we should think of it as an idyll. Reviewing a work of generic criticism, Margot Northey's *The Haunted Wilderness: The Gothic and Grotesque in Canadian Fiction*, Rosemary Sullivan offers two shrewd observations:

1) It is my bias that generic criticism must also be historical. Any analysis of a genre over two centuries cannot evade the responsibility of historical investigation. Furthermore the great vulnerability of generic criticism is its susceptibility to the niceties of cataloguing.
2) A healthy and mature criticism begins in the critical effort to order individual works into coherent patterns and to relate these in turn to the fabric of culture against which the notion of tradition becomes understandable.

To clear away the debris of indiscriminate rummaging among modes of expression about place, I suggest at least a beginning might be made by considering the ways in which writers themselves have seen their work as regional definitions, the difficult work of naming one's place and time.

The model for what I have in mind is in poetry, James Reaney's *Twelve Letters to a Small Town*, with its letter on "How to build a model of the town" and its unassertive search among metaphors of language, music, drama, and myth for the town's best image. Among prose works in English, a number occur to me as reflexive in this same way. Let me suggest their possibilities, not through any extended analyses of various texts, but rather by means of a schematic account of the sorts of boundaries employed and regions defined. This is an admittedly crude way of making the point that some works more clearly than others help to bring their forms and problems into focus. Say, as an absolutely arbitrary (perhaps mystical) choice, nine; whether that choice means one covers all possibilities, I can't say, or whether it gives at least the range of approaches to the regions of Canada I don't know.

A judge and a pedlar trade wise saws and tall tales about the Bluenoses and the Yankees. A rich man in the city dreams the idyllic life of a small town. An immigrant enters America and with a vision and a book journeys down river to where he has nothing and everything, returning wiser and poorer. A teacher takes seven trips across an increasingly mysterious and threatening landscape and snowscape home to his wife and child. A drylander's odyssey is told by a mad biographer who gets into the journey to talk about writing it. Visions of the birth of the west and the death of vision. How to write a novel called *The Diviners*. The Wasteland somewhere out west. A reporter dreams his way back to his dream life in a small town.

You will, no doubt, have recognized the works I'm caricaturing in this scheme. A number, of course, are scarcely fictions, let alone novels; but Thomas Chandler Haliburton's and Stephen Leacock's sketches, F. P. Grove's essays and pseudo-autobiography, whatever the author's intention, contain, not only intriguing formal possibilities for the writer of fiction, but equally the forms or boundaries of regions: colony as opposed to republic, order as opposed to anarchy, energy as opposed to sloth translated in the language, terms, and conditions of Nova Scotian life in Haliburton; the double contrasts of true and false America, Europe and America in Grove's story of transformation from European to North American man. For obvious reasons, boundaries are drawn clearly in works which intend definitions of society.

I'm less comfortable with the ways in which one can talk about formal regionalism in the contemporary novel. Kroetsch's *The Studhorse Man*, Laurence's *The Diviners*, and Nowlan's *Various Persons Named Kevin O'Brien* tend to allow structural features of their work to show, the ribs and skeleton of the novel very deliberately evident. This is not to say the more raw-boned the novel, the better. The felt texture of a life, in the end no doubt, says more to us of the novelist's *world* than form itself might ever do. But surely it is just in so far as Laurence's "world of Manawaka" is realized that she transcends it and "regional" no longer seems the right word.

I suppose Sheila Watson's *The Double Hook* and Wiebe's *The Temptations of Big Bear* offer the formidable difficulties, test cases (so to speak). It's not a very good solution to a critical puzzle to say the tense allusiveness of the one and the visionary mode of the other provide formal designs of the kind I have been speaking of here. By means of allusion, Watson's work displays (I use Sullivan's words here) "the fabric of culture against which the notion of tradition becomes understandable" but because it is a learned book, and in a Borgesian sense "a successful innovation," it is both part of the enduring patterns of Western culture *and* particular and local. Wiebe's Big Bear, as the title of his work tells us, is a prophetic figure tragically pinned between the imperatives of power and spirit, between pragmatic force and religious vision, the boundary that, implacable as the iron lines patterning a new land, defines the immutable difference between past and present.

Possibilities. Fiction is little more than that. Presumably each of you will fill in your own ballot. Ondaatje's artist-narrator says at the end of *Coming Through Slaughter*, "there are no prizes." He is right. There are no rules either; or maybe it's better to say the writer remakes them each time he or she writes. We, of course, find ourselves then beyond theory and begin again. This is simply to say the "regional" is a limitation as much as a definition. For just as there is an inescapable doubleness in the notion of a national literature so there is in the notion of a regional literature. Or, as Mordecai Richler, another of our regionalists, puts it, "to be a Jew and a Canadian. That is to emerge from the ghetto twice." Few today, as I understand it, feel comfortable with notions of universality, but writing (especially conceived in regional *or* national terms) surely belongs not only within its boundaries but to what is outside, whether that is writing itself or perceptual flow, the *mere* phenomena. Regional implies its limitations and a transcendence.

I don't propose to say *how* peculiarities occur, only that they do. So it is we think of lost places, remembered places — or beyond that — remembered self, a kind of memory, a kind of myth, and how it is oneself and one's time one seeks. *That* has been lost. In *The Diviners* certainly. Someone trying to get home, to be at home in this world, the writer endlessly trying to get back, to find his way back, to return or perhaps to reinvent his world. I think of John Newlove on the prairies: "Everyone is so lonely in this country that it's necessary to be fantastic . . . necessary to be fantastic / almost to lie."

There are those high lonely places where with Ondaatje's novel and poem I began. Familiar territory begins to assume strange shapes. I doubt that Wiebe and Ondaatje would agree they have been to the *same* place, sheer cliffs of mind, but the moral paradoxes of the spirit speak in both. Oddest of all, to have come there

116

by familiar homely ways. I suppose that is why our most familiar homely writer remains our best regionalist, or so I think. Grove, our representative writer as Kroetsch would have it, remains our most duplicitous: Grove/Greve. And in his simplest, plainest work, *Over Prairie Trails*, he is oddest and most peculiar. Familiar territory assumes strange shapes.

This stubborn incredible man, like Ulysses not to be trusted, a teacher driving his cutter home through the Manitoba winter, intrepid voyager on the seas, facing the wrath of the gods. "Once . . . the temperature being very close to fifty below zero, I saw, in a fearful snow-drift no more than six miles from Gladstone, the head of a horse sticking out of the snow, frozen stiff; and as, turning aside, I passed with a shudder, I saw a corner of the sleigh and the head of the driver who was still sitting upright in death." What curious habit of mind could transform such grotesqueness into material dramatic, symbolic, and philosophic in scope, into questions about imagination and one's place in the world? What still more curious habit of mind could leave us uncertain about that dead horse, that driver in death — truth or lie? And why, in either case, would he want to tell it as he did?

Appendix: A Note on the Distinction: National / Regional

I. Identity Arguments

This is obviously not the place in which to rehearse either theoretical puzzles or the history of attitudes about the purpose of literature in this country. It is probably sufficient to note that there is a widespread view that literature serves as a means of national identification and accordingly as a force for national unity. One form of this view implies an analogy between an individual or person and a body of literature. Literature is to the nation what the personality is to the person. It defines us by telling us "who we are." Another form of the same view sees literature as defining or arising out of place, therefore providing us with a picture, so to speak, of "where we are." A subtler elaboration of this second view postulates a social and causal relationship: literature is a product of society and accordingly a portrait, not of its external features, but of its very nature and mode of operation and existence, its processes, so to speak. The first is a kind of cultural Freudianism; the second, a literary geography; the third, a literary sociology. Taken together, they would constitute, as many indeed argue they do, a psychological, geographical, and sociological portrait of Canada and hence an image of its character and nature, invaluable for the intricately particularized sense of the felt life of the country, not only its general features, but its very texture.

II. Against Identity

Frye's influential criticism points to a number of objections which have been urged against the view that literature serves as a means of national identification. I cite these in a series of points here, for convenience:

1) There are serious objections to the present state of both sociological and cultural criticism of literature, most notably the lack of rigour, especially in the implied statistical argument in both.

2) The identification of a national psyche in literature depends on a kind of abstraction from literary works which denies the particularity of each work in its form and language.

3) No satisfactory account of a national identity has yet been developed, since any such account invariably does less than justice to the variety and complexity of national characteristics in Canada, if indeed any *national* characteristics can be isolated for attention.

4) To equate national identification with a body of literature is to claim a false unity: the equation implies a single cultural identity but in fact Canada is, at the very least, bicultural if not multicultural.

5) Frye's very important distinction between identity and unity should be noted here. Indeed, one could develop some very important distinctions by pursuing the implications of his various attempts to arrive at a satisfactory account of Canadian writing, whether to take account of it in a national, international, or regional context.

Note: If items three and four appear to be the same, I should point out the extent to which this sort of analysis depends on the distinctions of the kind made by Professor Morris Careless in his article "Limited Identities." Distinctions of "class," "region," and "ethnicity" might very well apply more adequately to the

118

problem of defining a Canadian character and situation than any concept of "national identity."

III. Regionalism

Among the many objections to the various kinds of criticism concerned with an approach to a national literature, or to the identification of literature and national character, or literature and national identity, the most important, by far, is that the approach may not do justice to ethnic, class, and regional distinctions in Canadian writing. More, it begins to appear, whatever the developments in ethnic studies and ethnic writing (I think particularly of the recent establishment of a *Journal of Ethnic Studies* and an Association of Ethnic Studies) or in a literature concerned with class-consciousness, the genuinely critical questions to which any group of this sort concerned with questions of national literature will have to address itself are questions of literary regionalism.

One major line of argument in this paper is that there is a variety of reasons for thinking of literary regionalism not as the concern with an autonomous world but as the definition of a series of social relationships, boundaries. It might be defined as a border-line art. In the national/regional distinction these considerations present themselves:

1) The country is conceived, for obvious reasons, within a traditional geographic framework as a series of geographical regions: The Atlantic Provinces, Central Canada, The West, The North, The West Coast.

2) Within this framework, a whole series of forces operates to provide identities and distinctions, on the one hand, and relationships on the other: cultural distinctions, linguistic distinctions, administrative or political distinctions — or boundaries. Often, the tendency is to think of the country simply as a group of regions (originally colonies) gathered together in a loose federation. But it is possible to think of their relationships in another way; that is, regions as functions of the nation.

3) Following the work of Harold Innis, some historians have thought of the country as the logical development of its technologies, existing, in the classic phrase, because of, not in spite of its geography. The West, then, as an example, takes its character as a region very largely through the implementation of a federal policy

expansionist and protectionist in thrust: the creation of a hinterland for the central metropolis. Regional identity is inseparable from a national policy that creates an area of tension, its definition within its tensions of immigrant or ethnic settlement, exploitation of land and people, even within the tensions between human structures and natural forces. Consider the difference between "North" conceived as "myth," or "North" as "ecosystem," or "North" as "area of resource development." The latter, a version of region or hinterland of the southern metropolitan area, implies an area of tension with the centre, even as it is developed by the centre.

4) In political, rather than economic, terms, our only national context, it is argued by historians like Ramsay Cook, is juridical, administrative. This is the political version of Frye's argument about literary regionalism. To put multicultural, bicultural considerations in ideological terms (to identify the nation by one culture rather than by political structure) threatens its existence. The national context is political; the regional is cultural.

5) Malcolm Ross speaks of "the broad design of our unique, inevitable, and precarious cultural pattern." He distinguishes it as "a pattern of opposites in tension." A significant element in that cultural design, we might well believe, is literary regionalism. A final matter: It may very well be that the traditional framework of regions is no longer adequate as a basis for discussion of Canadian society for a simple reason. It no longer exists. Canada is now to be understood as a region of the United States. The code word is "The Americanization of Canada."

Acknowledgements

The argument developed above owes a great deal to the knowledge and wisdom of Professor William Westfall of York University, with whom I have collaborated in a course on "Regions and Regional Cultures." My other debts will be immediately recognizable. The essay develops from my reading in the following:
Northrop Frye, *The Bush Garden: Essays on the Canadian Imagination*; Laurie Ricou, *Vertical Man/Horizontal World: Man and Landscape in Canadian Prairie Fiction*; E. K. Brown, *On Canadian Poetry*; Robert Kroetsch, "Unhiding the Hidden," *Journal of Canadian Fiction*, 3, No. 3 (Autumn 1974); "Uncovering Our Dream World," *Arts Manitoba*, 1, No. 1 (Jan. 1977); Ann Mandel,

"The Frontiers of Memory," *Laurentian University Review/Revue de l'Université Laurentienne*, 7, No. 1 (Nov. 1975); Rosemary Sullivan, "Self-Discovery," *The Canadian Forum*, June-July 1977; Henry Kreisel, "The Prairies: A State of Mind," in *Contexts of Canadian Criticism: A Collection of Critical Essays*, ed. Eli Mandel (Chicago: Univ. of Chicago Press, 1971).

MARIAN ENGEL

I'm not going to quarrel with Eli Mandel because I think his paper is excellent and unobjectionable, but it did give rise to some observations and of course I have to make some, anyhow. But it struck me while he was speaking that writers, real writers, amongst whom I have the arrogance to count myself, live in our own countries; we live in another country that I think is best labelled by the title of one of Ruth Nichol's books, *The Marrow of the World.* I don't know whether that country is the big white winter prairie, or the seaside, or the valleys of British Columbia, or the nitty-gritty industrial towns that I grew up in in Ontario. I think it's a much more generalized thing, but I think we're always, always, always, striving to find that supernatural and almost surreal place where we feel we belong. But our strivings start in that reality in which we were born and we add to that reality places to which we were taken as children, and we became composites very early in our lives. The Canadian reality is added to that if we are Canadians, and that is of course that this country is so big it inevitably has regions. It's a very, very big country and it must be chopped up into smaller pieces in order to be digested by the imagination at all. So the real dilemma is to reconcile the reality of the region that we belong to and the big eternity that we write in order to belong to. Our consciousness is formed in many places and I have been increasingly aware of this as I have travelled more and more, as I've read more and more in the literature of this country.

Mine happens to be an eastern, almost European-looking consciousness, and I certainly find now, living in Alberta, that there's a very great difference between my Ontario eastern consciousness and that of other people I talk to. And also I find that the European centre of my consciousness was shaped by very different European influences than those that were foisted upon the people that I meet. My orientation as far as Europe is concerned tends to be French and English, not because I'm French, but because I was taught French very early. Secondly, it tends to be Mediterranean. Now I meet a lot of people the European centre of whose consciousness is from farther north and farther east in Europe and that's fascinating. I had an itinerant childhood; my life was fragmented as far as place goes, though many of the places I lived in were places in Ontario. I'm told that I write well about place and I think often that I write about place so often, and about houses so often, because I'm looking for my home and I don't have one. But what I found out about writing about place in Canada is that all the places in Canada have their different qualities, their different smells, their different official orientations. I remember that once, for what I thought was a large sum of money, I was offered a job writing something for an Ontario government pamphlet about Ontario, and the thing was returned to me with a large cheque just to get rid of me, saying that my depiction of Ontario was dreary and history-ridden. The Bureau of Tourism was having nothing to do with that. I think my consciousness of Ontario was absolutely accurate, but it didn't suit the official consciousness. We have to take into account increasingly in this country official reality as well as imaginative reality.

There are many other varieties of regionalism. Just before I came up to sit on this platform and open my mouth I said to somebody, "My God! Whom do I represent? Women?" and someone said, "Yes, you're the token woman." And then I thought, "Am I woman? Am I writers? Am I Ontario? Am I what?" My other regions are my gender, and if you think that gender is not a region, try writing a novel from the other gender's point of view. I'm conditioned also by my species, by my race, by what they call the ethnic origin of that race. And I'm conditioned by the rootedness of my particular family in the nation in which I grew up. Now at various points in my career, I have had to choose various poisons from among these various elements that have predominated in the work that I have done. It is only by synthesizing that this can be done because I am sure the profound difference between novelists and critics is that a good critic is a good analyst, and a good novelist is a good synthesizer, and in order to reach that big eternity we have to synthesize all those elements in our selves so that we are compounded of many regions. We neglect the regions of our country at our peril. If only the geographical region predominates in our work we write smaller books than we would perhaps want to, but this doesn't say that it shouldn't be done. After all the map of the country is still being made. We cannot escape who we are. I'd like first of all to be human, but I also know that I'm an animal. I'm a female, I'm a Canadian, I'm a WASP, and I'm an Ontarian, and these categories get into my work and I neglect them at my peril. Because, though I would like to achieve some kind of universality and get up into that big eternity that's way above my head, I suspect that it's my humanity and my Canadianness that keeps me from disappearing into the hopeless, mythic, imaginary spiral where no one can reach me and I can't reach anyone.

Our regionalism is part of our humanity and the varieties of political and social, and human experience within a region I find absolutely fascinating, particularly on the Prairies, because the minds I meet are so alienated, correctly, from the Ontario WASP stereotype that was drilled into me as a child. The orientation is quite different; it's much freer from the European stereotype as the Ontario experience is free of it compared to that of the Maritimes. But fiction writers cannot live on that theorizing plane; we write *out of* another piece of our selves which we hope to make universal, *out of* our reality. And that is not to say that fiction is not reality, but it's not to say that fiction is reality either. It seems to me that the real dilemma is the point where fiction begins and reality leaves off, and the synthesizing of these two — that's the real dilemma rather than the dilemma of regionalism.

FRANK WATT

Eli Mandel's attempt has been to rehabilitate the term regionalism, and it has been a "magnificent" attempt. I agree with that term, but I think that you could argue that it was rather magnificently perverse, too. He found the term regionalism as a pejorative term, as a term of limitation, as a kind of insult, I suppose, and he brought it along very subtly, very effectively, very persuasively, to the point where he at last was able to apply it to all the books that he likes. I have a great deal of sympathy with that approach, but the cost is quite considerable. The cost really is to have to throw out most of the books that are usually called regional or have had some equivalent label attached to them. I'm not entirely sure at this point that you can't accomplish what Professor Mandel wanted to accomplish while still retaining for literary criticism the term regionalism as a descriptive term without any value judgements implied in it at all.

Just to make a brief comment also on what Marian Engel had to say: what she did, and perhaps Professor Mandel and she are moving along the same line because of this, was to take the term regionalism and stretch it to include the kind of writing, all the kinds of writing, that she could imagine being worth writing. I think I'd like to stick to the proposition that you can be a good writer without being a regionalist, just as you can be a good writer and a regionalist. It seems to me that we could come back to a conception, a critical term, that would be a little more useful than what we are going to get if we stretch the term to too great an extent.

I want to begin by asking three questions. These are simple questions, but I hope that they won't seem simple-minded. The problems involved in definition really could benefit from a little further probing. The three questions are: What is a region? Can a city be a region — if not, why not? Can Canada be a region?

What is a region, that is to say a region in this literary context? It is important and useful to distinguish between a region and a province — Professor Mandel alluded to this connection. A province by definition has a political organization — a region needn't and in fact usually doesn't have a political organization. Moreover, a province has, again by definition, a centre of power and authority that is outside itself; a region holds out the possibility of having its own centrality. (Quebec, as in many matters, may turn out to be the exception that proves the rule, because Quebec may turn out to be both a province and a region.) A region then is a geographical area first of all, large or small, with recognizable natural characteristics and with social, cultural, historical accretions that have grown up in interaction with the natural features, a territory which the human imagination can perceive as coherent and / or attempt to contain as coherent, as one place. The ism of regionalism is the theory that a particular region and its human interactions are not peripheral, but are central in importance and significance.

124

Can a city be a region? Well, obviously villages and small towns can be regions by this definition; that is, they can be geographical areas with recognizable natural as well as man-made characteristics where the human and the natural can interact in distinctive ways, and which the imagination feeds on and attempts to grasp and contain in a coherent pattern. But, for better or for worse, villages and small towns grow up to be cities, usually, and in our day of course that means that they grow up to be modern, industrial, technological communications centres. In doing so they tend to lose their distinctive characteristics, and their exposure to the influences of the natural world. They become homogenized, standardized, universalized. The aim of modern technological and industrial urbanism is the total domination of nature, not the interaction of the human and the natural. The aim is the obliteration of regional differences; the city is judged by how successfully it accomplishes this. The result is that all too familiar phenomenon deplored in so much contemporary literature: modern urban men, deracinated, history-less, herded and huddled in the lonely crowd, dulled, desensitized by rapid transportation and instantaneous communication. Anywhere is everywhere; everywhere is anywhere; Toronto is Tokyo, Moscow is Moose Jaw. This is why Morley Callaghan could say that in Toronto and in Montreal, despite the alleged differences between those two cities, people really think pretty much the same thoughts. Can a city be a region? Not if it's a city the mayor can boast about.

Now I come to the hardest question: can Canada be a region? That is, a territory with human accretions interacting with the natural in distinctive ways, a place that feeds the imagination and can be grasped as a coherent pattern, as a whole. At this point, I have a note for myself, which says here the argument gets pretty shaky. Raise your voice a little. Go out on a very long digression. And this is what I'm going to do right now.

I was rereading a book the other day — it's a book which I found surprisingly useful in accounting for the relation between Canadian nationalism and Canadian regionalism — Hugh MacLennan's *Seven Rivers of Canada*. These were the "rivers that made the nation": the Mackenzie, the Fraser, the Saskatchewan, the Red, the St. Lawrence, the Ottawa, the Saint John. An approximation of the geographical regions of this country — not all of them but a rough sketch. MacLennan in this book presents the familiar Harold Innis-Donald Creighton argument that these great river systems were the basis for the east-west-north communication network that linked the old colonial regions and opened up new ones from sea to sea, making the nation possible and preventing the parts from falling into the maw of the United States of America. MacLennan describes not only the geographical features, but the historical, the social, and cultural features of the regions and dwells on their amazing distinctiveness, which is the product, in part, of vast space and slow time — the continental realities of our early history. But MacLennan also points out the terrible paradox of this historical regionalism: it was the expanding network of communications that made it possible, the network that has been so changed in modern times by the aeroplane, the train, and now of course, radio and television and all the rest, rapid transit and instantaneous communication. The paradox lies in the fact that the same factors that created and protected the regions now threaten to destroy them before their distinctive potentialities have been fully developed and realized. For a slowly growing, deeply rooted, richly varied regional life modern technology is substituting a fast-moving, centralizing, universalized stream of communications. Anywhere is everywhere; everywhere is anywhere. Vast time and slow space, vast space and slow time are obliterated. We are left essentially with modern, abstract, generalized, urbanized time and place. MacLennan puts this painful understanding in a single, pregnant phrase: "The nation seems almost to have outtravelled its own soul."[1]

Some recent Canadian fiction is moved and inspired by this very same or a similar understanding. So, basically, to return to the third question, some writers, though the critics perhaps not as often, have understood that as yet Canada can not be a region. Canada is only an abstract, generalized, political reality to the imagination of its citizens and the artists working within its boundaries. It exists as its regions. That's why we are now seeing the phenomenon which could be called, for the sake of dramatic effect, if not of strict, scholarly truth, *the new regionalism*. I take it that this new regionalism is, in part, what Eli Mandel has been talking about — new, because it's not the regionalism of innocence, naïveté, or simplicity, the regionalism of *Anne of Green Gables* or *Jalna* or even perhaps of *Who Has Seen the Wind* and *The Mountain and the Valley*. It's not the regionalism of Ralph Connor, or Martha Ostenso, or F. P. Grove, who a few generations ago were breaking through into undiscovered regions and were

126

newly charting them from within, not the regionalism of those comfortably or energetically moving within their own particular region's boundaries. It's rather the regionalism, which I think Professor Mandel has described effectively, of borderline art — what is inside seen in relation to the context of what's outside the region; the regionalism of those who have certainly, I think, travelled literally or figuratively the soulless path that MacLennan is talking about and then have gone back to revalue and reassess. And who have discovered the possibility of centrality, meaning, importance, value, significance, in the regions they know best, which have fed their imaginations even when in many cases they didn't realize it at the time, places which they can now grasp as having a coherent pattern. There seems to be a shift of energy from the abstract, centralizing movement of Canadian nationalism, towards a more intense rediscovery of the regions which someday may make the nation. This shift is of course one of the reasons why we are here in Calgary in February, not perhaps in Toronto, or Montreal, or Ottawa, or in some other equally non-distinctive place.

Let me try to offer a few samples of the way it would be argued that the new regionalism has checked, and slowed up, and countered, and reversed the process of rapid transit and instantaneous communication, the rush toward a standardized, centralized, modern industrial, urban Canada. For the new realists write fiction which often tends to show a kind of communication which is difficult, gradual, perhaps stalemated, countered by questions of roots and values. Jack Hodgins' Spit Delany lives by a highway, it's true, but his home is an abandoned gas station, the best kind, and the road, if I remember rightly, doesn't lead anywhere — actually I think it leads into the Pacific Ocean, and then it points to the oceanic crack deep under water that with the slowness of cosmic time is gradually pushing Asia farther away, separating the continents. Spit Delany's most cherished possession is a steam locomotive (and you must remember that Vancouver Island is some distance beyond the last spike) but this steam locomotive obviously isn't going anywhere; it's a museum piece which he polishes and nurses, and in fact loves, static as it is. Margaret Laurence's Morag in a symbolic setting too familiar to need comment lives beside a river very unlike the fluent communication channels Hugh MacLennan writes about. Morag's river flows *both* ways. At one time we might have thought of Marian Engel as an urban novelist, even though her best book is in fact set on a Mediterranean island (and it features a bishop and a donkey, not an archivist and a bear). However, the spirit of the new regionalism has affected Engel's work as well, to the point where she felt obliged to travel to a region north of Toronto, and there invent a regional history, and provide a coherent setting: an island on a river which is, incidentally, too much of a backwater to serve industry and commerce very effectively. It's a region where it is possible for the human and the natural to interact in especially distinctive ways. Rudy Wiebe's *The Blue Mountains of China* has a memorable scene in which a young Mennonite man travels along the Trans-Canada Highway, but in this case, he's really not going anywhere, either, in the ordinary sense of that highway. He is on foot, carrying a cross somewhere between Calgary and Edmonton. He's passed by Cadillacs and motorbikes and he's on a slow quest for other values. In some ways the most useful item that I can draw attention to, though I have to warn you that it's in a rather different mood, is a scene in Robert Kroetsch's *Badlands*. Here we can see most obviously how the imaginative energy has shifted from the centre to the region so that this place, this *now*, that preoccupies the novelist has taken on importance, meaning, centrality. William Dawe, the hero of the novel, is drifting down the Red Deer River in the badlands of Alberta, no motive power at all for his boat and just a couple of rather ineffectual steering oars. He is travelling not through the present, or towards the future, but into the past, looking for dinosaur bones which the earth is excreting onto the riverside for him to collect and take back to civilization. At the point in his quest where this is about to happen, one of the members of the expedition looks around and says, "Where are we?" and William Dawe answers in a phrase that magnificently dramatizes the new regionalism's simultaneous sense of the centrality of its own place, and its complex awareness of what's around. "Where are we?" and Dawe answers, "Asshole of the world."[2] You can't really find a region more central than that.

Let me now try to answer briefly the question: Where is the Canadian novel going? Well I think it's going deeper and deeper into more varied, more particularized explorations of meaning in vital, regional settings. We haven't even begun to recognize the number and the variety and the richness of the regions that are only now really coming to light. That's one of the reasons why I object to equating province and region — every province is full of regions, some of which have not yet been discovered. And whether the settings are urban or regional, the novel is going to go into more ingenious, inventive, and desperate attempts to escape the physical and spiritual trap of the universal modern city.

NOTES

[1] Hugh MacLennan, *Seven Rivers of Canada* (Toronto: Macmillan, 1961), p. viii.
[2] Robert Kroetsch, *Badlands* (Toronto: new press, 1975), p. 243.

RUDY WIEBE

I am happy to follow Frank Watt because I disagree with him tremendously. I was simply going to say that either there is only regional literature or there is none at all, and today I would like to argue that there is no such creature as regional literature. There is only the individual writer's imagination, creating the world he can create, and to see in the Prairie region, in the often slapstick humour of W. O. Mitchell, the ribald irony of Robert Kroetsch, the hoary moroseness of Sinclair Ross, and the warmth and religious quests of Margaret Laurence, anything in common other than the commonalty of the human condition, is for me silly. This tendency succumbs to the pervasive scholarly temptation to force creative matter into patterns. Well, all human life has patterns, of course, and if you are very clever and you pick your points carefully enough, you can doubtless prove that a moose has a good deal in common with a toothpick. But at that point I contend that it won't matter much what that common matter is. It seems to me that when Professor Watt talks about the homogeneous city, he's exactly speaking to that matter — the homogeneity of cities is of no interest at all to fiction writers; their distinctives are of interest and there always are distinctives. The Holiday Inn is of no interest to the fiction writer, whether it be in Moscow or Moose Jaw.

The longer I look at the longer fiction I've written, I swear I can't recognize what's regional about it. Dick Harrison's study of Prairie writing, *Unnamed Country: The Struggle for a Canadian Prairie Fiction*, is an excellent book; the first chapter points out that when English travellers came to the prairie region they didn't

129

know that they were looking at any landscape, it didn't have any scenery, and when they finally got to the North Saskatchewan River valley, they suddenly discovered a landscape that they could relate with. The landscape, the region is in the eye of the beholder — two persons seeing the terrain do not see the same landscape at all. This is a marginal point made by a story I once wrote called, "Where Is the Voice Coming From?" The eye sees and the eye does not see, I can look at a page of a Chinese newspaper for example, and I will see exactly what a Chinese reader sees but I do not see anything really. I recognize nothing. This is the way it is with regions, it seems to me. To what region do I belong? My first novel concentrated on a peasant settlement in the northern parkland of Saskatchewan, my second on a contemporary fur trader in the Canadian shield and in the Arctic, my fourth on the Indians of the 1880s who roamed the entire centre of the North American plains, and my fifth on a mixed race of peoples who lived on those plains but whose leaders were involved in living and working from the buffalo plains of Saskatchewan to the capitals of the U.S. and Canada, and to the schools and mental hospitals of Quebec, and my third novel, why, it moves from prairie Manitoba to the steppes of the Ukraine, to ships at sea, to the concentration camps of Siberia and the mountains of Outer Mongolia, to the deserts of Paraguay, to the highways of Alberta. How regional can a writer actually get? The culmination of this regionalism is no doubt the work of Margaret Laurence: the Canadian regional prairie novel of Africa.

This discussion of regionalism is an artificial construct for the convenience of — you supply your noun — who will not grant literature what it demands to be: a journey into the heart and mind of any man or woman, a man or woman that the writer has fallen in love with, or in hate with, so powerfully that he or she cannot let that person go, and how often do we not fall in love with that which is so totally unlike our own experience and unlike ourselves, persons totally inappropriate to our own existence. As John Fowles has recently said in a newspaper interview, "Characters and even situations are like children or lovers for a novelist; they need constant caressing, concern, listening to, watching, admiring. All these occupations become tiring for the active partner, that is, the writer, and only something akin to love can provide the energy to do that." My love, my energy, I hope and pray, is as totally omnivorous as I pray my imagination could become. God save me from

130

any region or type that will limit me. I trust that I dare to look at God's good world anywhere, and that must be said of any true writer. I've been at enough conferences to simply state here that for heaven's sake don't box yourself into small compartments; the imaginations of the writers of this country, if they are worth listening to at all, *are their own places.* No writer worthy of the name writes from one simple place any more than he or she writes about one simple person. The world is the writer's place. The infinite complexities of humanity are his or her characters. To speak of geographical regionalism in a healthy literature is balderdash.

R. L. MCDOUGALL

I'm in favour of regions because I believe in boundaries. I think, in fact, that regions are here to stay. I can say that quite easily of geographical regions, of historical and political regions, certainly of social and personal regions. Peace to Professor Frye, I believe in literary regions, too, though I am impressed and indeed moved by what Rudy Wiebe has just been saying. He ended where I want to begin, with people. It seems to me we've been talking most of the time about the old temptress, the external world, the world that lies in heavy physical presence around us. And perhaps sometimes we even see people as objects against other objects or phenomena; but of course back of it all do lie human beings, characters; and human beings, characters, are the things that literature is supremely able to deal with.

It is now more than twenty years since Roy Daniells wrote an introduction to *As for Me and My House,* and he made two strange statements there, strange to me for a long time. "Most Canadian novels," he said, and you can sense the testiness in his voice a bit, "most Canadian novels worth reading suffer from a plethora of observed and recorded detail." And, as if that wasn't enough, he went on to say, "our prose is at present cumbered with detail and human documentation."[1] Now those words "plethora" and "cumbered" are strange, in a way. When Daniells used the term "human documentation," was he thinking of Buckler's *The Mountain and the Valley*, which came out about that time? Or was he thinking back as far as Raymond Knister, for example, in whose work, place begins to exercise some sovereignty over people, to erode and take away from them, to some extent? I do not know what Daniells had in mind here, but I do have a sense of a long contest in the novel between people and place. Place, of course, gives us Antaeus, whose story Coleridge liked, the man whose strength came when his foot was upon the earth, by extension in one place, for it could not be in many places at once. And yet, if we reinterpret the Antaeus story, or at least gloss it, Antaeus was destroyed by Hercules, uprooted and crushed in the air. He was a victim of undue reliance on place.

When the novel came along, it seems to me, it offered an exciting opportunity for opening up the definitions of place and time, because we now have a voice coming in, whether it's authorial or suspended in a character's point of view. One can get out and away from dramatic representation, which the drama had entailed, being in dialogue, and one can begin to flirt with this other thing. It's a costly but noble state of tension which develops here. Henry James, in *The Art of Fiction*, speaks of "solidity of specification," the supreme attribute on which the presence, the power of the novel, submissively depends. On the other hand, solidity of specification can run away with things, which it almost did (not quite) with James.

I recall an essay by Virginia Woolf:[2] her little feud with Arnold Bennett, the meaning of which is maybe not unlike what we're thinking about now. It's called "Mr. Bennett and Mrs. Brown," and Mrs. Brown is observed by Virginia Woolf sitting in the corner of a railway carriage compartment, and that's the Mrs. Brown Woolf keeps in mind and wants to know about. Now, she asks herself, what does Bennett do with a Mrs. Brown? Well, she quotes some passages from Bennett, who, in *Hilda Lessways*, has his Hilda standing at the window of her room looking out on the street, and there follows a long and meticulous description of the street, and then of the town, and the tax-rate system. "What of Hilda?" Woolf asks. Hilda stands at the window and we do not know much about her. Woolf says, "I have formed my own opinion of what Mr. Bennett is about. He's trying to make us imagine for him, he is trying to hypnotize us into the belief that because he has made a house, there must be people living there." And if we were to paraphrase that we might say that because there is a region, there must be a person or persons living there. It's a risky assumption.

It's an assumption, however, that lies behind some writing today, a "documentary" tradition being thrust upon us. Very often the background trespasses upon what should be absolutely foreground. There are novels of many kinds and some have leave of their own, and ask and get leave, to be horizontal, to go much that way. Others choose a vertical orientation. It came to me last night, listening to Brian Moore read. When Roy Daniells spoke of these things, I had a fair idea of what he was thinking in terms of the book he was introducing. He admired greatly the economy of Ross's novel — its spareness, its leanness, its refusal to be seduced by long and detailed "documentation." And so when I heard Brian Moore read last night, I heard a lean, economical narrative, focused where it should be, on a sufficient path of human relations. I cannot buy the argument that all the people in the region's cities and towns wear the region's marks. They wear masks, maybe, and place has something to do with these. They make it a little harder for the novelist to get inside people, but that makes the test all the more important. The eternal quest after the constant mystery of human consciousness and being: that is the supreme task of the novelist. Regions are great; but regionalism is a wily old temptress, I think to be resisted.

NOTES

¹ Roy Daniells, Introduction, in *As For Me and My House*, by Sinclair Ross (Toronto: McClelland and Stewart, 1957), pp. vii-ix.
² Virginia Woolf, "Mr. Bennett and Mrs. Brown," in *The Hogarth Essays* (New York: Doubleday, 1928), pp. 3-29. The text is that of a paper read to the Heretics, in Cambridge, England, on May 18, 1924.

DISCUSSION

The discussion for this fourth session continued the pursuit of a satisfactory definition for the apparently elusive concept of regionalism — without any striking consensus. Wiebe continued to protest adamantly against the term, but finally acquiesced to a suggestion that regionalism was not concerned with place, in spatial or geographical terms, but with the imagination, that it could be conceived of as an attitude of mind and heart, a fascination with place rather than place itself. This, however, was not satisfactory to a number of others who expressed a desire to retain the geographical dimensions of the concept. The discussion closed upon a debate concerning whether the term had pejorative implications, and concerning the place of autobiographical writing in this subject.

SESSION FIVE: Saturday Morning, February 18, 1978

Malcolm Ross: The Ballot
Panel
Henry Kreisel
Antoine Sirois
W. J. Keith
Discussion

135

The Ballot

MALCOLM ROSS

I would like to say a few words before the ballot is distributed. There has been, I think, some misunderstanding in what I am doing in all of this, and I didn't realize how much and how deep the misunderstanding was until I heard a CBC program called "Sunday Morning" a couple of weeks ago which astonished me. I was asked a few days later to give a response to this on the Eric Friesen show on CBC-FM — I don't think the same audience heard it, perhaps very few people here did, and I thought perhaps I should explain more precisely what I thought I was doing, by reading from my statement on that show.

"I heard the other day to my astonishment that one man, myself, had opened a Pandora's box of anger, gossip, and controversy. The remark had to do with a conference on the Canadian novel to be held at the University of Calgary. I had been invited by the conference to solicit a list of one hundred novels which could be used to illustrate a discussion of various critical problems. Much fun and fury has been inspired by the very notion of a list of books. The purpose and use of this list seems to have been quite misunderstood. For instance, it has been said, and quite properly, that literary criticism by ballot is not only impossible but invidious. It has been said that the frivolous parlour game of selecting books by ballot can result only in a mishmash of subjective choices and regional prejudices. I would not deny this. It has been said that I am trying to impose a fixed and definitive canon of one hundred novels on an innocent public, and that many a worthy novelist will be excluded, banished, deprived of a public, starved. Now the list is not a list of the one hundred greatest Canadian novels, or the ten greatest. I must explain (and this I think you all know, but I will read it) that at the conference there will be papers on contemporary standards, regionalism, the two cultures, and the thematic approach to the novel. The committee felt that our deliberations would be less abstract if they could be related to a reasonably representative list of books. I was asked to discover from my colleagues which one hundred Canadian novels seemed most useful in the classroom, and in a variety of courses, including courses concerned with cultural and social history. I consulted twenty specialists. My own New Canadian Library list of over one hundred titles was supplemented by them, and a list of two hundred novels was finally sent out to teachers and critics across the country. I asked for a choice of one hundred titles and a short list of ten novels which seemed most important — not great, mind you, *important*. Titles not on the ballot could be added, and, I'm sure, have been.

What do we hope to get from the ballot? The list should indicate at least the range of books now in general use. It may perhaps reveal gaps and omissions in our teaching and in our reading. It will probably contain titles which are little known but which perhaps should be known. I hope it will encourage publishers to make available books now out of reach. I hope it will encourage a wider interest in French-Canadian books in English and English-Canadian books in French. I hope it will make all of us more aware of the diverse regional values which should inform and enrich the Canadian imagination. But the list is tentative and merely experimental. I had not seen it until the day before yesterday, but whatever the results of the ballot, they will be subjected to rigorous scrutiny at the conference in the light of the major critical issues before the conference. I hope that from the discussion and the debate we will gain a more secure sense of what is really first-class in our fiction, and of what is important to us in assessing our own cultural development. I am confident that from experimental ventures such as this one at Calgary, we can widen the possibilities for the serious study of Canadian writing, create an interest in writers hitherto unread, and for the practising contemporary novelist, enlarge and enliven the reading public.''

I didn't have time when I made the preceding statement to suggest one other motive that the committee had in mind when it asked us to prepare this list. I think it was felt that by getting people to consider seriously before coming to the conference the books they were using, or perhaps should be using, that they would be better prepared for the kinds of discussions which we've had. It may be that there has been some subliminal effect of this preparation in what has already happened. I was interested myself in the process because of my own series, the New Canadian Library, which has just over one hundred titles. I was interested in discovering how many of them would survive this scrutiny, and I don't think it came out too badly. But I do hope we can take this list for what it is, a basis for discussion, a discussion which will attend to the major themes of this conference, and to the questions of what we do in our courses, of what we should do, of whether we are using the right materials, and of what materials we need to make accessible. Everyone will want to supplement these lists, or subtract from them, but I hope this can be done in the light of the issues of the conference, the major themes with which we began and with which, I hope, we shall end.

The purpose of the list of ten important books was to determine the difference between the general approval of a large number of novels, and a very careful, narrow selection. What I had in mind was this: are there any Canadian books which we could with confidence put on a course in contemporary fiction which would include writers like Patrick White, Saul Bellow, E. M. Forster; and what kind of authentic, rigid, severe standard can we apply to determine which novels would be suitable to such a context?

[At this point the lists were distributed.]

You will have noticed that these lists are not on tables of stone — that is the first thing that should be pointed out. I should also like to make a few remarks about some other aspects of this exercise. First, while there is obviously nothing conclusive about any such vote as this represents, it does confirm that we are no longer a nation of one-novel novelists: there are several works here by Gabrielle Roy, Margaret Laurence, Mordecai Richler, Marie-Claire Blais, Robertson Davies, Frederick Philip Grove, Morley Callaghan, Hugh MacLennan, Rudy Wiebe, and so it goes. We are developing writers who have size as well as quality.

Another consideration: has the presence of stars in our firmament now perhaps dimmed out, or made into distant galaxies, other luminaries who fade in their light? I don't have the complete statistical breakdown — I've been told we're all statisticians and accountants in this country, but if that is so, then I'm un-Canadian — but on the list you'll notice that the first novel of the one hundred is *The Stone Angel*, which was only two or three points ahead of *The Tin Flute*. The first ten or twelve novels were very closely ranked. By the time you get to *The Lives of Girls and Women*, the point total has dropped from 364 to 268; *Mad Shadows* stands at 219, *The Nymph and the Lamp* at 166, and, finally, *The Incomparable Atuk* at 118. I think it would be useful to read out a few more titles that were very close:

Matt Cohen	*The Disinherited*
Robert Kroetsch	*Badlands*
Brian Moore	*I Am Mary Dunne*
Morley Callaghan	*A Fine and Private Place*
Gwethalyn Graham	*Earth and High Heaven*
Sinclair Ross	*Sawbones Memorial*
Marie-Claire Blais	*The Manuscripts of Pauline Archange*
Fred Bodsworth	*The Last of the Curlews*
Gabrielle Roy	*Windflower*
Douglas Le Pan	*The Deserter*
Adele Wiseman	*Crackpot*
Earle Birney	*Down the Long Table*
Marie-Claire Blais	*Tête Blanche*
Edward McCourt	*Music at the Close*
Yves Thériault	*Ashini*
Marie-Claire Blais	*The Wolf*
Charles Bruce	*The Channel Shore*
Graeme Gibson	*Five Legs*
Mordecai Richler	*A Choice of Enemies*

Laura Goodman Salverson	*The Viking Heart*
F. P. Grove	*The Yoke of Life*
Ernest Buckler	*The Cruellest Month*
Réjean Ducharme	*The Swallower Swallowed*
Henry Kreisel	*The Betrayal*

Now all these run within just one or two points of each other, and in no significant way behind the last twenty of the list of one hundred — and so it keeps going. There are several aspects of this pattern to consider. Recent important publications would not normally appear on such a list as this because they have not circulated in the cheaper paperback editions. A good example is Jack Hodgins' *The Invention of the World*, which has been mentioned several times in the course of this conference, but which didn't get enough support because there has not yet been time for it to be widely read. The same is true of Ondaatje's *Coming Through Slaughter* and Oonah McFee's *Sandbars*. A similar problem faces young writers such as David Richards, whose stars will rise in time, especially when their work has had an opportunity to circulate in paperback. A list such as this cannot be definitive because it cannot represent writers such as these.

I was glad to see, among some of the earlier novels, Sara Jeannette Duncan's *The Imperialist* do extremely well. I was puzzled to see *Maria Chapdelaine* written in, and *Wolf Willow* appearing nowhere. *Wolf Willow* is as much Canadian as *Maria Chapdelaine*, surely.

Problems and limitations similar to those just mentioned attach to the list of ten important books. Close behind *The Diviners* comes *The Imperialist*, Leacock's *Sunshine Sketches of a Little Town*, and Lowry's *Under the Volcano*. The last obviously is a novel that ranks high in world fiction, but many people didn't vote for it because they thought it could not be called a Canadian novel. Others take the same view of Brian Moore's works. Moore is in a difficult position lately: he's ineligible for the American Academy of Arts because he's a Canadian citizen, and he's looked upon as an alien by many Canadians because he lives part of the year in California. Immediately after Lowry come:

Alice Munro	*Lives of Girls and Women*
Margaret Atwood	*Surfacing*
Mordecai Richler	*St. Urbain's Horseman*

Ringuet	*Thirty Acres*
Leonard Cohen	*Beautiful Losers*
Marie-Claire Blais	*A Season in the Life of Emmanuel*
Hugh MacLennan	*Two Solitudes*
Morley Callaghan	*The Loved and the Lost*
Rudy Wiebe	*The Temptations of Big Bear*
Ethel Wilson	*Swamp Angel*
Adele Wiseman	*The Sacrifice*
A. M. Klein	*The Second Scroll*
Robert Kroetsch	*The Studhorse Man*

These are obviously strong books and there are many more that came close to these and that belong in their company.

The final list I will mention very briefly. It is interesting to see the *Literary History of Canada* far up out of the range of all of the others; it is an indispensable book for anyone undertaking serious study of our literature. But others did very well:

Irving Layton	*Selected Poems*
A. J. M. Smith	*The Book of Canadian Poetry*
Eli Mandel	*Contexts of Canadian Criticism*
Desmond Pacey	*Creative Writing in Canada*

So, I'll close my remarks by reiterating my insistence that this list is not meant to be definitive. It is meant to be a basis for a discussion that I hope will reflect and pull together some of the discussions we have already had.

One final issue. There are fewer French-Canadian titles even in the NCL than one would expect to see (we have about twenty-five), but one reason for this early on was lack of translation, and then another problem developed: many Departments of English do not teach novels in translation because Departments of French want to do them in their own language. I'm not sure what the answer is. There is a concerted effort just beginning, supported by the Canada Council, to make available each year, in both languages, six or seven major titles. This will be done quite systematically, they will be carefully chosen, and I think some good will come of it.

I am replacing Robert Kroetsch, whose name has been pronounced variously throughout this conference. My name too has been subjected to such variety. And so I suggested to Kroetsch yesterday that the man who should be here is Robert Henry Kröesel, and so he is. Now this Kröesel's mind contains a lot of absolutely useless bits of information that rattle around in the nooks and crannies of that mind, and one of those absolutely useless bits of information is the name of the first winner of the Nobel Prize in Literature, in 1901. Now presumably in 1900 the Swedish Academy sat down, after sending ballots around the world, to wrestle with the momentous problem of who should be chosen to be the first winner of the Nobel Prize — the whole world waiting breathlessly. In 1900-01, as you may remember, Leo Tolstoy was living, Anton Chekhov was living, Henrik Ibsen was living, August Strindberg was living, Thomas Hardy was living — others also were living, but these people certainly were living. Now, you would have thought that it would be a difficult choice having these names before them, but when the name was announced, the winner was René-François-Armand-Sully-Prudhomme. He was a French poet, even then not a truly major figure, but more major than now. Anyway, Sully-Prudhomme was the first winner of the Nobel Prize for Literature.

As I said, this is one of the bits of bric-a-brac that rattles around in Kröesel's mind. Kröesel is terrified by lists. *Time* announces the most essential one hundred books in world civilization. He rushes down to get his copy because he wants to satisfy himself that he's a well-read fellow; he knows and wants to have his superiority confirmed. He looks at the list, and of the one hundred he knows two. Great depression sets in. He rushes to the library to take out an eight-volume epic of a sixteenth-century Japanese poet which he must read, looks at the nineteenth-century hexameters into which it is translated and decides he can spend the rest of his life without benefit of the sixteenth-century Japanese epic.

So there's the question of lists, you see, and of rating and ranking. We all know that literary reputations are not built and perpetuated by any lists. Malcolm Ross knows this, we all know it, and yet we like to play the game. Human beings are drawn to making lists. We all make lists, of all kinds, because it gives us the

142

sense that we've mastered something, controlled it, put fences around it. I look at lists. I'm drawn to lists, like anybody else, but I remember Sully-Prudhomme and the sixteenth-century Japanese epic that I will never read — even some of the great works of western literature that I will never read. I used to feel guilty about that, but I've come to terms with it. One will survive somehow.

I didn't know there was a ballot of two hundred titles; Kreisel wasn't asked to fill it out . . . Kröesel was certainly not asked. I got this only yesterday and looked at it, looked naturally at the first ten novels — the first ten of the hit parade — the titles I suppose will be announced and pronounced, and maybe even the rock stations will play the first ten. But I looked at it seriously, and these are names that I would have expected to see on such a list. My own choices of books might be different, but the names would be there. I would put F. P. Grove's *Over Prairie Trails* there because I think that's his best book. I would put Mordecai Richler's *Son of a Smaller Hero* on, rather than *The Apprenticeship of Duddy Kravitz*, but I can see why *The Apprenticeship* is on. The first ten constitute a respectable list. These are names that I would certainly recommend to people asking what to read. I'm always being asked. I spent some time in Cambridge a little while ago, and a number of people, believe it or not, are becoming interested in Canada, and they asked me what writers one should read, and I think I mentioned all of the ten listed here. I mentioned other people as well, probably because I know them and they write on subjects I know. I mentioned Rudy Wiebe and others. No one can argue that these ten be mentioned at some time.

The C list surprises me more. I notice that it stipulates various genres, and some of the novels that have already been listed, are listed here. I am quite surprised not to see Marshall McLuhan, an influential thinker certainly, and one who has had an impact, whatever debates one might have with him. He's a major figure, and that he is not here is surprising. Harold Innis also might be on such a list. Although he is not as well known, he is the intellectual father of McLuhan and one of the central thinkers about the nature of Canada. I would put on *The Gutenberg Galaxy*, though others might prefer *Understanding Media*.

For the rest, it is surprising, in a way, that there are one or two hundred novels that one can list. I don't think that would have been possible fifteen or twenty years ago. I also believe that quality is absolutely essential, but I think that you get quality because you have

143

quantity. You don't get one play by Shakespeare alone; there's a whole milieu in which he created, and there are other great peaks, and lesser peaks, and small ranges. You have to create an atmosphere, a climate of opinion in which creation becomes possible. And if one approaches this list in the spirit in which, as Malcolm Ross explained, it has been made, it can be useful. One can debate, one can disagree, as certain people do, disagree strongly with the whole concept of making lists, and that's all right, though the very fact that one talks about something, renders it important. I think the list can have a useful function . . . as long as one always remembers Sully-Prudhomme.

ANTOINE SIROIS

I have the feeling that I am carrying the whole of French-Canadian literature on my fragile shoulders. But my remarks will bear in mind one of the important purposes of this conference, "to provide a norm that can serve as a curricular reference for courses in Canadian literary studies." It is extremely difficult to establish a final criterion in judging literature. There were norms for the novel at the time of Victor Hugo, new norms after with Honoré de Balzac, other norms with James Joyce, still other norms with the *nouveau roman*, and further new norms with Réjean Ducharme. These criteria are relative, belonging to different periods, and varying with the appearance of a few geniuses and also with the evolution of society which has, with different periods, different ways of receiving literary creations.

We have a very young literature. It is not more than one hundred and fifty years old and has a life of its own — I should say of their own, because we could speak of at least two literatures. They slowly evolved from under the domination of the old countries, France and England. They then developed in rapid stages, under many other influences, and in close connection with the social and political evolution of Canada. They were also punctuated in their evolution by such events as Confederation, the two World Wars, the Depression, and the awakening of a new nationalism.

The books we want to choose for a curriculum depend very much on our aims. If we have in mind a survey course linked to literary history, novels might be chosen according to different periods, according to their genres, according to movements, or according to their forms. Novels might be chosen to illustrate history or psychology, to analyze themes, or for their originality or formal inventiveness. So we have to make choices according to our aims and from a young literature still in evolution, and we cannot always expect to find a masterpiece for all the purposes we have in mind, however good these literatures have begun to be.

The list has of course missed some very important French-Canadian novels, primarily because many of them have yet to be translated. Even so, there are several which should be more prominently placed: Hubert Aquin's *Prochain épisode*, Germaine Guèvremont's *Le Survenant*, Gérard Bessette's *Le Libraire*, Réjean Ducharme's *L'Avalée des avalées*, among others. As for *Maria Chapdelaine*, please forget it. Louis Hémon was born in France, lived in France and England, stayed a few years in Quebec, and died in Ontario.

W. J. KEITH

The appropriate title for today's seminar is the title of this afternoon's movie: *Why Rock the Boat*. The original plan for this panel was that the four main speakers from the previous sessions should form it. I am the sole survivor; perhaps I'll go down with the ship. So be it. Yesterday I named names, I survived. Here more names are named; I may not survive, but the names will. These will be controversial. Canadian literature can survive controversy — it may even thrive on it. I hold no brief for this list. I "wrote in" twenty-two of the one hundred that I chose. I don't think any of them got on. But I would like to make a few points about my position.

I did not fill in C: the first ten works of various genres. That seemed to me impossible. The results make me feel justified. Four out of the ten works are, for goodness' sake, criticism, and however good the criticism may be, that, as Rudy Wiebe said yesterday on another matter, is balderdash. I have doubts about the first ten. I could not distinguish between those and a lot of others. The A section is all right, as long as you don't take it too seriously. Mordecai Richler was quoted in *The Albertan* this morning as saying that this was amusing. W. O. Mitchell said something like, "O.K. but surely nobody's taking it seriously, are they?", and I said something similar — none of us knew what the others had said, but surely that was the right way to take the list. If I may be so bold as to criticize the conference organizers, biting the hand that feeds me, I think the list is poorly titled: "Results of Ballot on Significant Canadian Novels and Other Genres" — it isn't that. It's a list of what a possibly random cross section of teachers, critics, commentators, etc., considers to be one hundred significant novels. It has a certain value in a psychological sense perhaps, or in a sociological sense, perhaps even in a literary-historical, if not literary-critical, sense.

I would like to support Professor Sirois' remarks. I think it's important that an English-Canadian should say it. I would like to dissociate myself from the way Québécois texts were treated. The titles in English translation give away that particular show. I tried to suggest yesterday that we, and I mean for the moment English-speaking Canadians, are not very good at responding to style and language in our own language, and if I may be specific and naughty about this, as I work down the list I see John Richardson's *Wacousta* in front of Rudy Wiebe's *The Temptations of Big Bear*. *Wacousta* may be interesting thematically; *The Temptations of Big Bear* is important as a work of art. How on earth, then, having seen this, can we — unless we are fully bilingual, and not many of us are — make a value judgement about Québécois fiction, whether we read it in translation or stumblingly in French?

I am, however, prepared to approve moderately, without taking it too seriously, the tentative drawing up of such a list. Mention has been made of the top ten — I am such a natural highbrow that I don't know anything about the top ten, except this — that the top ten never stays the top ten for very long. The main reason for approving moderately is that some such evaluation, some such list, is going to be made anyway, and let us not deceive ourselves about that. If we as critics of and commentators upon literature do not make our presence felt, do not stand up to be counted, then the list is going to be made up by others whom I would be even more reluctant to see making it. It will be made, first, by publishers who make the decisions anyway, and it's only right that they should — remember what Douglas Gibson from Macmillan said on Thursday: they must make the decisions, and it is magnificent that there are times, as in the case of *The Invention of the World*, when the decision is not made solely in terms of dollars and cents, at least in the short run. But if we convince them that our judgements must be considered, the list won't be any worse, and it might be a lot better. Again, if we don't, the other people who are going to make the decisions are the handful of reviewers on the larger newspapers, and, frankly, I have doubts about their judgement. And, most sinister of all, the decision is going to be made by those who control what goes on the shelves of the proliferating chain book stores. We are going to get, if we haven't got it already, and I think we *have* got it already, the kind of store across this country for which decisions will be made by some centralized administrative person in one of those wicked places like Toronto or, worse, New York. In that system the local manager has no control over the books that he must sell. If we can do anything to put a spoke into that, this conference will have justified itself.

This list, then, seems to me a beginning, a tentative beginning, a crude beginning. There are a number of books, doubtless, that are not there which should be there — and the converse is obviously true. That will in time be righted. That is how literary criticism works; it is a collaborative enterprise. Some I know are uneasy about this, to put it mildly. I suppose I'm uneasy too, but not much, because I just don't take it seriously. Let me explain. Who remembers now the first words of the first paper of this conference? I remember them: "F. R. Leavis." Leavis' main critical principle is as follows: It is a critic's function to say "This is so, isn't it?" The next critic's function is to say "Yes, but . . . ," or perhaps, "No, not at all . . . ." Leavis begins *The Great Tradition: George Eliot, Henry James, Joseph Conrad* by saying, and Kroetsch quoted it, that the great tradition of the English novel consists of Jane Austen, George Eliot, Henry James, Joseph Conrad, and D. H. Lawrence, and on second thought, twenty years later, he added Dickens. He did not say, "No other novelists count." A lot of people think he said that, and Kroetsch may have implied that he did, but Leavis never said that.

This list does not say that other novels do not count. It says, "These are significant novels, aren't they?" And each of us must say "Yes, but . . . ," or perhaps, "No, not at all." Criticism, Leavis said, is essentially collaborative. There is no academy, there is no list fixed for eternity. We are human, and we argue, and we play games, as Kreisel said. Why not argue about books? It's a start, perhaps a poor one (especially as far as Québécois fiction is concerned).

I now want to say one provocative thing, then one tactful thing. Some are concerned that the list will be accepted as gospel, especially by beleaguered high-school teachers. Well, if the present gospel is Atwood's *Survival: A Thematic Guide to Canadian Literature*, then at least we can't do worse in offering a new one. Yesterday I argued for something to balance the present emphasis on thematic criticism — today I see this list as possibly useful in providing a balance to *Survival*'s influential, too influential, list of recommended readings. But let me end on a less petulant note, the tactful note, pouring Alberta oil on troubled waters. I've heard it said that people will read this list and decide that novels not on it need not be read. I do not believe that. I have faith in the quality of Canadian fiction. I have faith in the vast majority of works on this list, and in a large number that didn't make it. If someone reads the books on this list, will he or she stop there? Certainly not. He or she will certainly say that this has not closed down a subject, but has opened it up: "If this is a sampling of Canadian fiction, I want more."

DISCUSSION

The final discussion of the conference was a spirited affair, and ranged widely, touching on several issues raised by the panelists. Several speakers agreed that French-Canadian literature had not been properly represented by the ballot results, and John Lennox of York University put forward two resolutions: (1) that more money be provided by the Canada Council for translation; (2) that it be recommended to the different bodies of education in this country that education in the French language be reinstated. Notice of these motions was favourably taken, although there was no machinery to give them formal authority.

Marian Engel pointed out that the list revealed that "the books that are taught are books that are published in paperback form, principally in the two series that keep paperbacks in print," and exhorted all teachers to "keep in mind the fact that the small presses like Anansi, new press when it existed, and others, have been the promulgators of an extraordinary range of new Canadian literature, and unless you keep their catalogues in mind as well as the standard lists when you are ordering for teaching, you will be doing a great disservice to the new literature that is being created."

The observation was also made that the list reconfirmed with its relative inattention to nineteenth-century works that "we have rejected this period too long in our studies."

Beyond these specific deficiencies, however, a profound general unease with the entire list-making exercise was expressed. This ranged from the statement that "the committee has done Canadian literature a very great disservice by putting out such a list," to the concern of John Moss and Barry Cameron as to the list's future, its potentially damaging authority. Malcolm Ross, in reply to Moss, *again* reiterated that it was never intended that the list enjoy any such authority, and exhorted the media not to distort matters by suggesting that the list bore any such stamp of academic or conference approval. Eli Mandel, nonetheless, forcefully dissociated himself completely from what he termed "a genuine Canadian document," both "balanced" (symmetrical) and "unbalanced," a "blue paper," "anonymous," and "prepared in a very Canadian way, by a committee." Mandel concluded by quoting Matthew Arnold again, "The only thing a man of culture should say when he's called before a committee is what Socrates said, "Know Thyself.' "

A number of other speakers agreed with W. J. Keith that the lists should not be taken seriously. Most prominent of these speakers was Margaret Laurence, who began the session's discussion by saying:

> I'd just like to make clear that I didn't vote on that ballot; politicians may vote for themselves, but I'm not a politician. I think probably many, or perhaps all of my fellow writers, would share my deep doubts about the possibility of making up a list of ten because when I think of the books on that list, I immediately want to add more — Rudy Wiebe's *The Temptations of Big Bear* and Adele Wiseman's *The Sacrifice* spring to mind at once. I agree with what Henry Kreisel, in his new persona, had to say. I have a feeling that being on a list like that is the surest way to getting on a fast train to oblivion.

But as my dear friend Adele Wiseman once said to me, "Kid, we're not in it for the immortality stakes."

So, a list of ten is probably not possible, but a list of one hundred, so long as it is not taken too seriously, is a very interesting game. It's a very worthwhile game, simply because these are books which are significant in the teaching of Canadian literature in our high schools and in our universities. Obviously, it cannot be a definitive list in any way; we are not in the business of embalming a fly in amber. This list is going to be open-ended; it will have to be added to and altered constantly. It's a working list and interesting in that respect. I profoundly agree with William Keith when he said that any kind of list of this nature is not going to close down on the reading of Canadian literature, but will rather tend to open it up. Anybody who reads through this list will want to read more.

This is an open thing and should be so regarded; it's an interesting working list, in no way definitive, but something to be getting on with.

APPENDIX

The lists below were the results of a mail ballot completed before the conference began. As Malcolm Ross noted, lists of Canadian fiction and works in other genres were distributed to Canadian "teachers and critics," who were invited to choose 1) the most "important" one hundred works of fiction (List A); 2) the most important ten novels (List B); and 3) the most important ten works of various genres (List C).

Several conference participants were careful not to claim too much importance for the ballot; their comments appear in the text. At least two participants, Eli Mandel and Ronald Sutherland, dissociated themselves entirely from the entire process of the vote. Mandel's reasons are reported briefly in the record of the discussion following Session Five. Sutherland's objections are as follows: "I feel that the ballot to determine the 'hundred best Canadian novels' was an unfortunate and misguided gimmick and that the decision of ECW PRESS to publicize it further is a disservice to

Canadian writing. While a number of the books which got onto the list are of established and undoubted merit, many others are there simply because of the availability of texts (mainly from the New Canadian Library Series) or of translations (creating a sadly distorted picture of Quebec authors)."

List A (author and title)

Roy	*The Tin Flute*
Richler	*The Apprenticeship of Duddy Kravitz*
Ross	*As for Me and My House*
Davies	*Fifth Business*
Leacock	*Sunshine Sketches of a Little Town*
Buckler	*The Mountain and the Valley*
Mitchell	*Who Has Seen the Wind*
MacLennan	*The Watch That Ends the Night*
MacLennan	*Two Solitudes*
Laurence	*The Diviners*
Lowry	*Under the Volcano*
Haliburton	*The Clockmaker*
Watson	*The Double Hook*
Richler	*St. Urbain's Horseman*
Ringuet	*Thirty Acres*
Hémon	*Maria Chapdelaine*
MacLennan	*Barometer Rising*
Munro	*Lives of Girls and Women*
Carrier	*La Guerre, Yes Sir!*
Atwood	*Surfacing*
Callaghan	*Such Is My Beloved*
Grove	*Settlers of the Marsh*
Laurence	*A Jest of God*
Wiseman	*The Sacrifice*
Duncan	*The Imperialist*
Hébert	*Kamouraska*
Wilson	*Swamp Angel*
Klein	*The Second Scroll*
Grove	*Fruits of the Earth*
Callaghan	*The Loved and the Lost*
Cohen	*Beautiful Losers*

Grove	*The Master of the Mill*
Davies	*The Manticore*
MacLennan	*Each Man's Son*
Richardson	*Wacousta*
Wiebe	*The Temptations of Big Bear*
Laurence	*The Fire-Dwellers*
Davies	*World of Wonders*
Kroetsch	*The Studhorse Man*
Montgomery	*Anne of Green Gables*
Blais	*Mad Shadows*
Callaghan	*More Joy in Heaven*
Ostenso	*Wild Geese*
Roy	*Where Nests the Water Hen*
Roy	*The Cashier*
Kirby	*The Golden Dog*
Blais	*A Season in the Life of Emmanuel*
Atwood	*The Edible Woman*
Callaghan	*They Shall Inherit the Earth*
Moore	*The Luck of Ginger Coffey*
Brooke	*The History of Emily Montague*
Davies	*Leaven of Malice*
Lemelin	*The Town Below*
Aquin	*Prochain épisode*
Connor	*The Man From Glengarry*
Moore	*Judith Hearne*
Roy	*Street of Riches*
Birney	*Turvey: A Military Picarèsque*
Grove	*A Search For America: The Odyssey of an Immigrant*
de la Roche	*Jalna*
Thériault	*Agaguk*
Grove	*In Search of Myself*
Richler	*Son of a Smaller Hero*
Davies	*A Mixture of Frailties*
MacLennan	*Return of the Sphinx*
Engel	*Bear*
Stead	*Grain*
De Mille	*A Strange Manuscript Found in a Copper Cylinder*
Godfrey	*The New Ancestors*
Raddall	*The Nymph and the Lamp*

Cohen	*The Favourite Game*
Roy	*The Hidden Mountain*
Wiebe	*Peace Shall Destroy Many*
Kreisel	*The Rich Man*
Wright	*The Weekend Man*
O'Hagan	*Tay John*
Marlyn	*Under the Ribs of Death*
Atwood	*Lady Oracle*
Carrier	*Floralie, Where Are You?*
Lowry	*Hear Us O Lord From Heaven Thy Dwelling Place*
Roy	*The Road Past Altamont*
Lemelin	*The Plouffe Family*
Laurence	*This Side Jordan*
Callaghan	*Close to the Sun Again*
Carrier	*Is It the Sun, Philibert?*
Parker	*The Seats of the Mighty*
Knister	*White Narcissus*
Roberts	*The Heart of the Ancient Wood*
De Gaspé	*Canadians of Old*
Wiebe	*The Blue Mountains of China*
Langevin	*Dust Over the City*
Raddall	*His Majesty's Yankees*
Wilson	*The Innocent Traveller*
Godbout	*The Knife on the Table*
Hood	*White Figure, White Ground*
Kroetsch	*The Words of My Roaring*
MacDougall	*Execution*
Connor	*Glengarry School Days*
Richler	*The Incomparable Atuk*

List B (author and title)

Laurence	*The Stone Angel*
Davies	*Fifth Business*
Ross	*As For Me and My House*
Buckler	*The Mountain and the Valley*
Roy	*The Tin Flute*
Richler	*The Apprenticeship of Duddy Kravitz*
Watson	*The Double Hook*

153

MacLennan	*The Watch That Ends the Night*
Mitchell	*Who Has Seen the Wind*
Laurence	*The Diviners*

List C (author and title)

Klinck	*Literary History of Canada: Canadian Literature in English*
Frye	*The Bush Garden: Essays on the Canadian Imagination*
Pratt	*Collected Poems*
Leacock	*Sunshine Sketches of a Little Town*
Jones	*Butterfly on Rock: A Study of Themes and Images in Canadian Literature*
Moodie	*Roughing It in the Bush; or, Forest Life in Canada*
Atwood	*Survival: A Thematic Guide to Canadian Literature*
Laurence	*The Stone Angel*
Ross	*As for Me and My House*
Birney	*Collected Poems*

APPENDIX

When the Conference Organizing Committee was designing the structure of its sessions, the decision was made to attempt to define a more specific and wider *corpus* of novels than the incidental delimitation of theme papers could provide. Such a *corpus*, we felt, would provide a more specific context for, and would thereby help to point more effectively, the conference discussions. The committee learned that Professor Malcolm Ross was interested in evaluating, by means of polling educators, book reviewers, and literary critics, the efficacy and utility of the implicit canon of Canadian fiction established by his New Canadian Library series. The committee decided to ask Professor Ross to construct his poll to accommodate our somewhat more general interests, and to report his results to the Conference. He agreed.

We had initially planned to begin the Conference with Professor Ross's report. Considerations of a rather dramatic media response prompted the fear that the ballot results might deflect attention from the more important papers, panels, and discussions, and perhaps even distort some of these into wranglings about rankings. These fears, tempered by the expectation that Professor Ross's information would be too valuable to be completely ignored (a conviction which I hold even more strongly now), moved the committee to reschedule his report to the final day of the conference.

The above accounts of the conference's final session represent to some degree the rationale for the ballot exercise as a whole, and for the specific structures of the individual ballots. In an attempt to clarify these even further, we include here the texts of: (A) the Conference Committee's letter to prospective panelists; (B) Professor Ross's letter accompanying the distributed ballots; and (C) the "Official Ballot for the Selection of Canadian Novels."

Charles R. Steele
Editor

155

(A) Letter to the Panelists

The University of Calgary Library, in conjunction with the Department of English, the Humanities Institute, and the Faculty of Humanities, is sponsoring a "Conference on the Canadian Novel" to be held February 15, 16, 17 and 18, 1978. This conference will bring together major Canadian writers, critics, and publishers in discussions relating to this literary form. The conference, incidentally, has been greeted enthusiastically by a number of funding agencies including the Arts Council and the Humanities and Social Sciences Council of the Canada Council.

The specific objectives of the Conference are as follows:

1) To focus on the Canadian novel and to determine for the first time novels which have established themselves as major works, or Canadian classics. The purposes here are to provide a norm that can serve as a curriculum reference for courses in Canadian literary studies in educational institutions; to suggest direction for publishers of Canadian fiction series; to establish selection criteria for future scholarly editions of Canadian novels; and finally, to provide a guide to Canadians as a whole who are interested in the masterworks of their Canadian literature.

2) To bring together major Canadian novelists and critics in order to focus attention on our literary heritage. In stating that objective it is recognized that most nations in the world are identified with their national literature.

3) To encourage an interest in creative writing and Canadian literature and to give students from western Canada a first-hand opportunity to celebrate their Canadian literary heritage and meet informally with noted writers and scholars.

4) To publicize the richness of our literary heritage with ancillary activities such as readings, author interviews, a major book fair and a festival of films based upon Canadian novels.

The conference program will be composed of five sessions:

1) Contemporary Standards in the Canadian Novel;
2) Regionalism and the Canadian Novel;
3) Themes in the Canadian Novel;
4) The Two Cultures in the Canadian Novel;
5) The Major Canadian Novels.

These themes have been chosen as convenient vehicles to recapitulate and discuss the "state-of-the-art" or the direction of literary scholarship to date. The first session, for example, will serve to introduce the conference and will discuss, in general terms, present and expected standards for this literary form. The remaining papers, within their specific terms of reference, will examine criteria upon which the selection of significant novels should be based. They will, moreover, suggest and justify particular titles indicative of such criteria. The papers would be followed by panel and general discussions which would permit reflection upon or disputation of the criteria or titles. The final and key session, organized by Malcolm Ross, will attempt to synthesize the discussion which has preceded, and examine, in the light of a pre-conference ballot of selected Canadian literature experts, the selection criteria and specific titles to be considered as the most significant of Canadian novels.

(B) Letter with the Ballot

Dear Delegate:

As you know the University of Calgary is organizing a national Conference on the Canadian Novel to be held in Calgary February 15-18, 1978. It will be the aim of the Conference to examine the diversity, quality and availability of appropriate texts of Canadian novels for use in the classroom and for scholarly research. It is also hoped that the Conference will be able to propose a list of significant Canadian novels that can serve as a guide to those interested in the masterworks of our literary tradition.

As a full session of the Conference will be devoted to a discussion of a list of novels which can be recommended as central to any study of Canadian literature, I have been asked to solicit, in advance of the meeting, the considered views of all those who are being invited to attend the Conference: your recommendations will be tabulated and the results presented to the Conference for full discussion.

As an aid to memory and to facilitate the recording of your choices, I have drawn up a preliminary list of about 200 titles. I am asking you to select one hundred works and to rate them by placing a mark in one of the three ballot boxes beside each item. I am also requesting that you write in, in the lines provided at the end of the list, any novels which are not listed but which you feel should be added to a tabulation of significant Canadian novels.

Because I am viewing these titles partially from the perspective of teaching Canadian literature, I have felt justified in including some works of historic or developmental interest. Although such works may not always be up to the same literary standard as other novels, they are important for a full understanding of Canadian literature and the various directions it has taken. There are other anomalies. The inclusion of Leacock's SUNSHINE SKETCHES is a case in point. Although this is not a novel in the formal sense, it has been important in the study of Canadian fiction and hence is represented here.

I now come to a second request. Would you, on the sheet provided below, list your choices for the *ten* best Canadian novels yet written?

And, if I may beg your indulgence still further, would you list on the last sheet the ten Canadian works of literature *of any genre* (including literary criticism) which you consider most indispensable to the study and appreciation of our national literary heritage?

No one is more sensitive than I am to the demands made upon one's time by requests of this kind. I trust that you will feel the issue urgent enough to respond. And I would be most grateful if you could return the ballot to me by January 8th, 1978, in the stamped and addressed envelope provided.

(C) "Official Ballot for the Selection of
Canadian Novels"

NATIONAL CONFERENCE ON THE CANADIAN NOVEL

Calgary, February 15~18, 1978

Official Ballot for the Selection of
Canadian Novels

NOVELS

CATEGORIES

Author	Title	Major	Significant	Of Secondary Importance
AQUIN, Hubert	THE ANTIPHONARY	☐	☐	☐
	BLACKOUT	☐	☐	☐
	PROCHAIN EPISODE	☐	☐	☐
ATWOOD, Margaret	THE EDIBLE WOMAN	☐	☐	☐
	LADY ORACLE	☐	☐	☐
	SURFACING	☐	☐	☐
BACQUE, James	BIG LONELY	☐	☐	☐
BERESFORD-HOWE, C.	THE BOOK OF EVE	☐	☐	☐
BESSETTE, Gerard	NOT FOR EVERY EYE	☐	☐	☐
BIRNEY, Earle	DOWN THE LONG TABLE	☐	☐	☐
	TURVEY	☐	☐	☐
BLAIS, Marie-Claire	MAD SHADOWS	☐	☐	☐
	TETE BLANCHE	☐	☐	☐
	THE MS. OF PAULINE ARCHANGE	☐	☐	☐
	THE WOLF	☐	☐	☐
	A SEASON IN THE LIFE OF EMMANUEL	☐	☐	☐
BLAISE, Clark and MUKHERJEE, Bharati	DAYS AND NIGHTS IN CALCUTTA	☐	☐	☐
BLONDAL, Patricia	A CANDLE TO LIGHT THE SUN	☐	☐	☐
BODSWORTH, Fred	LAST OF THE CURLEWS	☐	☐	☐
	THE STRANGE ONE	☐	☐	☐
BROOKE, Frances	THE HISTORY OF EMILY MONTAGUE	☐	☐	☐
BRUCE, Charles	CHANNEL SHORE	☐	☐	☐
BUCKLER, Ernest	THE CRUELEST MONTH	☐	☐	☐
	THE MOUNTAIN AND THE VALLEY	☐	☐	☐
BUTLER, Juan	CABBAGETOWN DIARY	☐	☐	☐
	THE GARBAGE MAN	☐	☐	☐
	CANADIAN HEATING OIL	☐	☐	☐
CALLAGHAN, Morley	SUCH IS MY BELOVED	☐	☐	☐
	MORE JOY IN HEAVEN	☐	☐	☐
	THEY SHALL INHERIT THE EARTH	☐	☐	☐
	THE LOVED AND THE LOST	☐	☐	☐
	A FINE AND PRIVATE PLACE	☐	☐	☐
	CLOSE TO THE SUN AGAIN	☐	☐	☐
CARRIER, Jean-Guy	MY FATHER'S HOUSE	☐	☐	☐
CARRIER, Roch	LA GUERRE, YES SIR!	☐	☐	☐
	FLORALIE, WHERE ARE YOU?	☐	☐	☐
	IS IT THE SUN, PHILIBERT?	☐	☐	☐
CHILD, Philip	GOD'S SPARROWS	☐	☐	☐
	THE VILLAGE OF SOULS	☐	☐	☐
	MR. AMES AGAINST TIME	☐	☐	☐
COHEN, Leonard	THE FAVOURITE GAME	☐	☐	☐
	BEAUTIFUL LOSERS	☐	☐	☐
COHEN, Matt	THE DISINHERITED	☐	☐	☐
	COLUMBUS AND THE FAT LADY	☐	☐	☐
	WOODEN HUNTERS	☐	☐	☐
CONNOR. Ralph	THE MAN FROM GLENGARRY	☐	☐	☐
	GLENGARRY SCHOOL DAYS	☐	☐	☐
CREIGHTON, Luella	HIGH BRIGHT BUGGY WHEELS	☐	☐	☐
DAVIES, Robertson	LEAVEN OF MALICE	☐	☐	☐
	A MIXTURE OF FRAILITIES	☐	☐	☐
	FIFTH BUSINESS	☐	☐	☐
	THE MANTICORE	☐	☐	☐
	WORLD OF WONDERS	☐	☐	☐
DAY, Frank Peter	JOHN PAUL'S ROCK	☐	☐	☐
DE GASPE, Philippe A.	CANADIANS OF OLD	☐	☐	☐
DE LA ROCHE, Mazo	JALNA	☐	☐	☐
	POSSESSION	☐	☐	☐
DE MILLE, James	A STRANGE MANUSCRIPT FOUND IN A COPPER CYLINDER	☐	☐	☐
DOUGALL, Lily	THE MERMAID	☐	☐	☐
	WHAT NECESSITY KNOWS	☐	☐	☐

NOVELS

CATEGORIES

Author	Title	Major	Significant	Of Secondary Importance
DEWDNEY, Selwyn	WIND WITHOUT RAIN	☐	☐	☐
DREW, Wayland	THE WABENO FEAST	☐	☐	☐
DUCHARME, Rejean	THE SWALLOWER SWALLOWED	☐	☐	☐
DULEY, Margaret	HIGHWAY OF VALOUR	☐	☐	☐
	GREEN AFTERNOON	☐	☐	☐
DUNCAN, Norman	THE WAY OF THE SEA	☐	☐	☐
DUNCAN, Sara Jeannette	THE IMPERIALIST	☐	☐	☐
	COUSIN CINDERELLA	☐	☐	☐
	A SOCIAL DEPARTURE	☐	☐	☐
	THOSE DELIGHTFUL AMERICANS	☐	☐	☐
	AN AMERICAN GIRL IN LONDON	☐	☐	☐
	A DAUGHTER OF TODAY	☐	☐	☐
	HIS HONOUR AND A LADY	☐	☐	☐
ELLIOTT, George	THE KISSING MAN	☐	☐	☐
ENGEL, Marian	BEAR	☐	☐	☐
	THE HONEYMAN FESTIVAL	☐	☐	☐
EVANS, Hubert	MIST ON THE RIVER	☐	☐	☐
FERRON, Jacques	ST. ELIAS	☐	☐	☐
FRASER, Sylvia	PANDORA	☐	☐	☐
	THE CANDY FACTORY	☐	☐	☐
FRASER, William A.	BLOOD LILIES	☐	☐	☐
	LONE FURROW	☐	☐	☐
GALLANT, Mavis	THE PEGNITZ JUNCTION	☐	☐	☐
GALT, John	BOGLE CORBET	☐	☐	☐
GERIN-LAJOIE, Antoine	JEAN RIVARD	☐	☐	☐
GIBSON, Graeme	FIVE LEGS	☐	☐	☐
	COMMUNION	☐	☐	☐
GODBOUT, Jacques	KNIFE ON THE TABLE	☐	☐	☐
GODFREY, David	THE NEW ANCESTORS	☐	☐	☐
	DEATH GOES BETTER WITH COCA COLA	☐	☐	☐
GRAHAM, Gwethalyn	EARTH AND HIGH HEAVEN	☐	☐	☐
GRAINGER M. Allerdale	WOODSMEN OF THE WEST	☐	☐	☐
GREY, Francis W.	THE CURE OF ST. PHILIPPE	☐	☐	☐
GROVE, Frederick P.	THE MASTER OF THE MILL	☐	☐	☐
	FRUITS OF THE EARTH	☐	☐	☐
	SETTLERS OF THE MARSH	☐	☐	☐
	THE YOKE OF LIFE	☐	☐	☐
	A SEARCH FOR AMERICA	☐	☐	☐
	IN SEARCH OF MYSELF	☐	☐	☐
	CONSIDER HER WAYS	☐	☐	☐
GUEVREMONT, Germaine	THE OUTLANDER	☐	☐	☐
HALIBURTON, Thomas Chandler	THE CLOCKMAKER	☐	☐	☐
HARLOW, Robert	SCANN	☐	☐	☐
HEBERT, A.	KAMOURASKA	☐	☐	☐
	CHILDREN OF THE BLACK SABBATH	☐	☐	☐
HEMON, Louis	MARIA CHAPDELAINE	☐	☐	☐
HODGINS, Jack	THE INVENTION OF THE WORLD	☐	☐	☐
HOLMES, A. S.	BELINDA	☐	☐	☐
HOOD, Hugh	WHITE FIGURE, WHITE GROUND	☐	☐	☐
HORWOOD, Harald	WHITE ESKIMO	☐	☐	☐
HOUSTON, James	THE WHITE DAWN	☐	☐	☐
JANES, Percy	HOUSE OF HATE	☐	☐	☐
KIRBY, William	THE GOLDEN DOG	☐	☐	☐
KLEIN, A.M.	THE SECOND SCROLL	☐	☐	☐
KNISTER, Raymond	WHITE NARCISSUS	☐	☐	☐
KREISEL, Henry	THE RICH MAN	☐	☐	☐
	THE BETRAYAL	☐	☐	☐

NOVELS

CATEGORIES

Author	Title	Major	Significant	Of Secondary Importance
KROETSCH, Robert	THE STUDHORSE MAN	☐	☐	☐
	THE WORDS OF MY ROARING	☐	☐	☐
	BADLANDS	☐	☐	☐
LANGEVIN, Andre	DUST OVER THE CITY	☐	☐	☐
	ORPHAN STREET	☐	☐	☐
LAURENCE, Margaret	THE FIRE-DWELLERS	☐	☐	☐
	THE STONE ANGEL	☐	☐	☐
	A JEST OF GOD	☐	☐	☐
	THIS SIDE JORDAN	☐	☐	☐
	THE DIVINERS	☐	☐	☐
LEACOCK, Stephen	SUNSHINE SKETCHES OF A LITTLE TOWN	☐	☐	☐
LEMELIN, Roger	THE TOWN BELOW	☐	☐	☐
	THE PLOUFFE FAMILY	☐	☐	☐
LE PAN, Douglas	THE DESERTER	☐	☐	☐
LEPROHON, Rosanna	ANTOINETTE DE MIRECOURT	☐	☐	☐
LEWIS, Wyndam	SELF-CONDEMNED	☐	☐	☐
LOWELL, Robert Traill Spence	NEW PRIEST IN CONCEPTION BAY	☐	☐	☐
LOWRY, Malcolm	UNDER THE VOLCANO	☐	☐	☐
	HEAR US O LORD	☐	☐	☐
LUDWIG, Jack	ABOVE GROUND	☐	☐	☐
MACLENNAN, Hugh	RETURN OF THE SPHINX	☐	☐	☐
	BAROMETER RISING	☐	☐	☐
	EACH MAN'S SON	☐	☐	☐
	TWO SOLITUDES	☐	☐	☐
	WATCH THAT ENDS THE NIGHT	☐	☐	☐
MACDOUGALL, Colin	EXECUTION	☐	☐	☐
MACPHAIL, Sir Andrew	THE MASTER'S WIFE	☐	☐	☐
MARLYN, John	UNDER THE RIBS OF DEATH	☐	☐	☐
MCCOURT, Edward	MUSIC AT THE CLOSE	☐	☐	☐
	THE WOODEN SWORD	☐	☐	☐
MEADE, Edward	REMEMBER ME	☐	☐	☐
MITCHELL, W.O.	WHO HAS SEEN THE WIND	☐	☐	☐
MONTGOMERY, L.M.	ANNE OF GREEN GABLES	☐	☐	☐
MOORE, BRIAN	THE LUCK OF GINGER COFFEY	☐	☐	☐
	JUDITH HEARNE	☐	☐	☐
	I AM MARY DUNNE	☐	☐	☐
MUKHERJEE, Bharati	WIFE	☐	☐	☐
MUNRO, Alice	LIVES OF GIRLS AND WOMEN	☐	☐	☐
MYERS, Martin	THE ASSIGNMENT	☐	☐	☐
NIVEN, Frederick	THE FLYING YEARS	☐	☐	☐
O'HAGAN, Howard	TAY JOHN	☐	☐	☐
OSTENSO, Martha	WILD GEESE	☐	☐	☐
PAGE, P.K.	THE SUN AND THE MOON	☐	☐	☐
PARKER, Gilbert	THE SEATS OF THE MIGHTY	☐	☐	☐
RADDALL, Thomas H.	ROGER SUDDEN	☐	☐	☐
	PRIDE'S FANCY	☐	☐	☐
	HIS MAJESTY'S YANKEES	☐	☐	☐
	THE NYMPH AND THE LAMP	☐	☐	☐
	THE WINGS OF NIGHT	☐	☐	☐
	HANGMAN'S BEACH	☐	☐	☐
RICHARDS, D.H.	BLOOD TIES	☐	☐	☐
RICHARDSON, John	WACOUSTA	☐	☐	☐
	THE CANADIAN BROTHERS	☐	☐	☐
RICHLER, Mordecai	SON OF A SMALLER HERO	☐	☐	☐
	THE APPRENTICESHIP OF DUDDY KRAVITZ	☐	☐	☐
	THE INCOMPARABLE ATUK	☐	☐	☐
	A CHOICE OF ENEMIES	☐	☐	☐
	ST. URBAIN'S HORSEMAN	☐	☐	☐

NOVELS

CATEGORIES

Author	Title	Major	Significant	Of Secondary Importance
RINGUET	THIRTY ACRES	☐	☐	☐
ROBERTS, Sir Charles	THE HEART OF THE ANCIENT WOOD	☐	☐	☐
	THE HEART THAT KNOWS	☐	☐	☐
ROBERTS, Theodore G.	THE HARBOR MASTER	☐	☐	☐
	THE RED FEATHERS			
ROSS, Sinclair	AS FOR ME AND MY HOUSE	☐	☐	☐
	SAWBONES MEMORIAL	☐	☐	☐
ROY, Gabrielle	THE TIN FLUTE	☐	☐	☐
	WHERE NESTS THE WATER HEN	☐	☐	☐
	THE CASHIER	☐	☐	☐
	STREET OF RICHES	☐	☐	☐
	THE HIDDEN MOUNTAIN	☐	☐	☐
ROY, Gabrielle	WINDFLOWER	☐	☐	☐
	THE ROAD PAST ALTAMONT	☐	☐	☐
SALVERSON, Laura G.	THE VIKING HEART	☐	☐	☐
	CONFESSIONS OF AN IMMIGRANT'S DAUGHTER	☐	☐	☐
SERVICE, Robert	THE PRETENDER	☐	☐	☐
SHIELDS, Carol	SMALL CEREMONIES	☐	☐	☐
SIMPSON, Leo	THE PEACOCK PAPERS	☐	☐	☐
STEAD, Robert J.C.	GRAIN	☐	☐	☐
STRINGER, A.	PRAIRIE WIFE	☐	☐	☐
SYMONS, Scott	PLACE D'ARMES	☐	☐	☐
THERIAULT, Yves	AGAGUK	☐	☐	☐
	ASHINI	☐	☐	☐
WALKER, David	WHERE THE HIGH WINDS BLOW	☐	☐	☐
WALLACE, F.W.	BLUE WATERS	☐	☐	☐
WATSON, Sheila	THE DOUBLE HOOK	☐	☐	☐
WIEBE, Rudy	PEACE SHALL DESTROY MANY	☐	☐	☐
	THE BLUE MOUNTAINS OF CHINA	☐	☐	☐
	THE TEMPTATIONS OF BIG BEAR	☐	☐	☐
WILSON, Ethel	SWAMP ANGEL	☐	☐	☐
	THE INNOCENT TRAVELLERS	☐	☐	☐
WISEMAN, Adele	THE SACRIFICE	☐	☐	☐
	CRACKPOT	☐	☐	☐
WRIGHT, Richard	THE WEEKEND MAN	☐	☐	☐
YORK, Thomas	WE, THE WILDERNESS	☐	☐	☐